BLACK & DECKER.

THE COMPLETE GUIDE TO

PAINTING *and* Decorating

CREATIVE PUBLISHING international

MINNETONKA, MINNESOTA

www.howtobookstore.com

Contents

President/CEO: David D. Murphy
VP/Editor-in-Chief: Patricia K. Jacobsen
VP/Retail Sales & Marketing:
  Richard M. Miller

Library of Congress Cataloging-in-Publication Data
The complete guide to painting & decorating.
       p.   cm.
     --At head of title: Black & Decker.
     ISBN 0-86573-632-4 (softcover)
     1. House painting. 2. Interior decoration. 3. Paperhanging.
I. Black & Decker Corporation (Towson, Md.) II. Creative Publishing
International. III. Title: Complete guide to painting and
decorating. IV. Title: Black & Decker. V. Title: Black & Decker
the complete guide to painting & decorating.
TT323.C66   1999
698' . 14--dc21
                                                99-23622

Advanced Painting & Decorating

Page 156

Executive Editor: Bryan Trandem
Creative Director: Tim Himsel
Managing Editors: Jennifer Caliandro,
  Michelle Skudlarek
Senior Editor: Jerri Farris

Editors: Christian Paschke, Philip Schmidt
Art Directors: Gina Seeling, Kevin Walton
Project Manager: Michelle Skudlarek
Mac Designers: Patricia Goar, Lynne
  Hanauer, Jon Simpson
Technical Photo Editor: Keith Thompson
Photo Stylists: Arlene Dohrman, Bridget
  Haugh, Joanne Wawra
Photo Researcher: Angie Hartwell
Hand Model: Kay Wethern
Photo Services Manager: Marcia
  Chambers
Photo Services Coordinator: Carol
  Osterhus
Photo Team Leader: Chuck Nields
Photographer: Jamie Mauk

Scene Shop Carpenters: Gregory
  Wallace, Dan Widerski
Production Services Manager: Kim Gerber
Production Staff: Stasia Dorn, Laura
  Hokkanen, Helga Thielen

THE COMPLETE GUIDE TO PAINTING &
DECORATING
Created by: The Editors of Creative Publishing international, Inc., in cooperation with
Black & Decker. **BLACK&DECKER.** is a trademark of the Black & Decker Corporation
and is used under llicense.

Portions of *The Complete Guide to Painting
& Decorating* were previously published in
Decorating With Paint & Wallcovering.

Other books offered from this publisher include:

*Decorating With Paint & Wallcovering,
Carpentry: Tools • Shelves • Walls •
Doors, Remodeling Kitchens, Basic
Wiring & Electrical Repairs, Workshop
Tips & Techniques, Advanced Home
Wiring, Carpentry: Remodeling, Land-
scape Design & Construction, Bathroom
Remodeling, Built-In Projects for the
Home, Refinishing & Finishing Wood,
Exterior Home Repairs & Improvements,
Home Masonry Repairs & Projects,
Building Porches & Patios, Flooring
Projects & Techniques, Advanced Home
Plumbing, Complete Guide to Home
Wiring, Complete Guide to Home Plumb-
ing, Complete Guide to Decks, Complete
Guide to Home Masonry, Complete
Photo Guide to Home Repair*

Introduction

The Complete Guide to Painting & Decorating contains all the information you need to turn every room of your home into a beautifully decorated living space. The 700 full-color photographs and concise, do-it-yourself instructions illustrate professional painting and decorating techniques. The book is divided into three easy-to-follow sections that cover everything you need to know about painting and decorating: Color & Decorating Principles, Basic Painting & Wallcovering, and Advanced Painting & Decorating.

Beginning with Color & Decorating Principles, you will learn about color theory and how to choose color schemes that suit your room and appeal to your tastes. This section explains in detail the effects of colors, the different types of color schemes, and the varieties of patterns. You will discover how to use color and pattern to create a mood in a room and how to finalize a room design.

The next section, Basic Paint & Wallcovering, illustrates step-by-step methods professionals use to paint and wallcover walls and ceilings. This section explains how to make necessary repairs and preparations to ensure a flawless finish for paint or wallcovering. The basic painting techniques walk you through the painting process, from choosing paint and equipment, to applying the paint and cleaning up. Similarly, the basic wallcovering techniques cover the processes of choosing wallcovering, estimating quantities, and selecting tools and materials, as well as preparing and hanging wallcovering.

The final section of the book, Advanced Painting & Decorating, demonstrates how to embellish walls and floors with faux finish designs and decorative accents commonly used by professional artisans. Information on choosing specialty painting tools and preparing paint glazes, combined with detailed instructions, help you create these stunning finishes yourself. The advanced decorating projects include methods for adding an elegant touch to walls with wallcovering cutouts, cornices, and wall frame moldings. This section also features a surprisingly simple method for transforming rooms with stunning crown moldings and ceiling medallions made from a polyurethane product that resembles plaster.

Color & Decorating Principles

Understanding Color

Although some people know instinctively how to choose effective color combinations, the majority of us need to rely on color theory to select colors that enhance our homes.

Basic color theory is illustrated with a color wheel. The color wheel shows how colors, also called *hues,* are related. The colors on the color wheel are classified as either primary or secondary. Combinations of these colors are described as either related or complementary, based on their position on the color wheel.

Red, yellow, and blue are primary colors. Orange, green, and purple are secondary colors, made by combining two primary colors. All paint colors are created from some combination of white, black, and primary colors.

Basic Color Theory

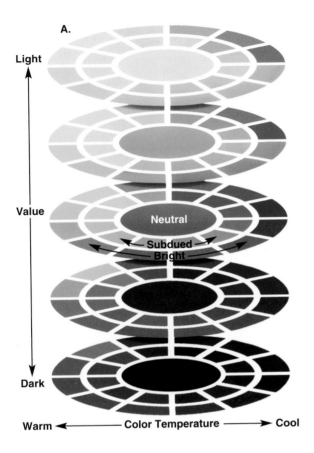

A.

Light

Value

Neutral

Subdued ← →
Bright

Dark

Warm ← Color Temperature → Cool

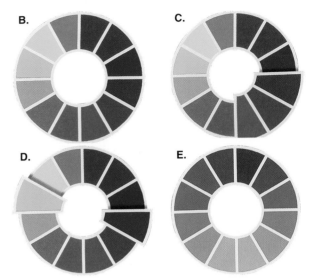

A: The dimensions of color are illustrated with these variations of the color wheel. Colors range in value, brightness, and temperature. All colors are made from some combination of white, black, and primary colors. **B:** The color wheel illustrates how the basic colors are related. **C:** Related colors are those next to one another on the color wheel. **D:** Complementary colors are located opposite one another on the color wheel. **E:** Neutral colors are shades of white, grey, or beige.

Related colors are those next to one another on the color wheel. For example, red and orange are related colors.

Complementary colors are located opposite each other on the color wheel. Blue, for example, is the complement of orange.

Neutral colors are shades of white, gray, or beige. Most neutrals are tinted slightly with another color.

Colors are also classified by their value, saturation, and temperature. In this section, you will learn about how each of these properties affects the way we respond to colors.

The *value* of a hue is determined by the amount of white or black present and is expressed in terms of a color's lightness or darkness. Light colors have a greater percentage of white; dark colors contain more black.

Saturation describes the brightness of a hue. Saturated hues, also called bright colors, are intense hues that are undiluted by black, white, or a complementary color. Desaturated colors, also called subdued colors, are formed when a hue is diluted with white, black, or a complementary hue.

Colors are also described as being either *warm* or *cool*. Warm hues are variations of red, orange, yellow, and brown; cool hues are variations of green, blue, and purple.

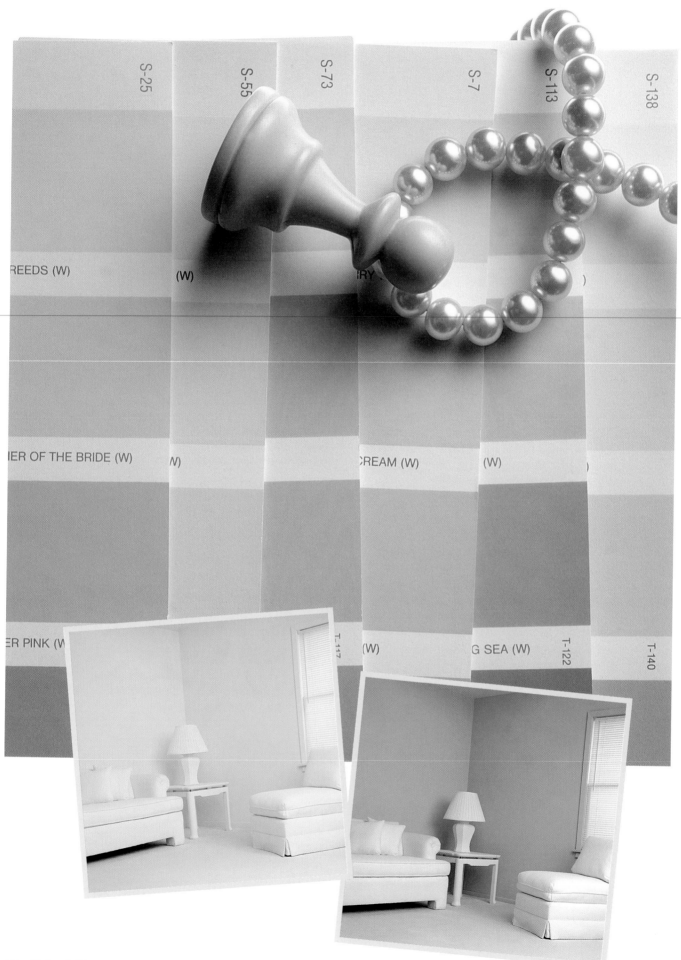

S-25

S-55

S-73

S-7

S-113

S-138

REEDS (W)

(W)

RY

ER OF THE BRIDE (W)

W)

CREAM (W)

(W)

ER PINK (W

T-117

(W)

G SEA (W)

T-122

T-140

Light Colors

*L*ight colors help create bright, spacious-feeling rooms. To the eye, light colors seem to recede, making rooms appear larger and ceilings higher. Since light colors reflect light well, they can brighten a north-facing room, a closet, or dark hallway.

Whites and other light colors are good choices for a nursery or a child's bedroom. In any room, white walls form a neutral background that does not compete with furnishings.

Wall roughness and paint sheen can affect the lightness of any color. Smooth surfaces and gloss paints reflect maximum light to make a color seem lighter. Rough-textured walls and flat-sheen paints hold more shadow and minimize the lightness of a color.

Opposite: Light colors reflect light, which makes rooms appear larger and more open. In these rooms, the light furnishings blend with the walls to increase the feeling of openness. Use light wall colors in small rooms or in rooms with little natural light.

Below: Light colors help to brighten a decorating scheme.

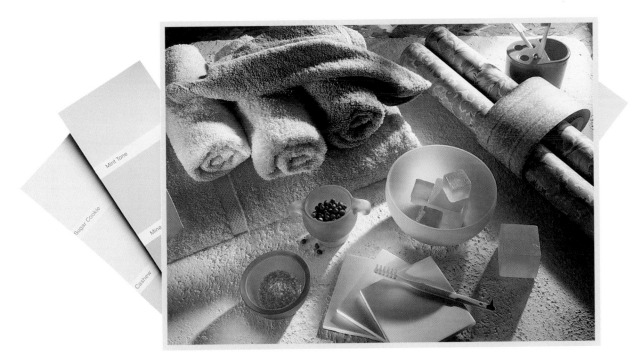

8 TH 9 GINGER PINK (W) T-28 T-65 T-117 (W) G SEA (W) T-122

8 TH 10 CICELY (M) E (W))) CK (W)

) ESS SEA (M)

8 TH 12 M EE S-25

Dark Colors

Use dark colors to create an intimate room. Because dark colors absorb light, walls appear closer and make the room seem smaller. Dark colors are most often used in libraries, studies, and other quiet areas.

Dark colors can be used to disguise problem areas, such as uneven walls, or to make a high ceiling seem lower. In heavy-use areas, dark colors can hide wear. Rough surfaces and flat-paint finishes make colors seem darker because they absorb more light.

Dark walls tend to dominate, so you may want to use lighter-colored accents to add balance to a dark room.

Opposite: Dark-colored walls in these rooms emphasize the light furnishings. Dark-colored furnishings would blend into this type of room, creating a heavier atmosphere.

Below: Using rich, jewel-toned dark colors creates a quiet, elegant setting.

50 TH 20 GOLDEN YE

50 TH 21 LIBERT

50 TH 22 NA

50 TH 2

50 TH 7 CARMINE (R)

50 TH 8 CINDER RED

50 TH 9 SIRO

50 TH 14 ORANGE FLIP (O)

50 TH 15 JUICY FRUIT (O)

50 TH 16 EARTH TILE (U)

50 TH

50 TH 17 BRIGHT ORANGE (O)

Warm Colors

Reds, yellows, browns, oranges, and peaches are warm colors. Intense warm colors create exciting spaces, while subdued warm colors form pleasant rooms for social gatherings. Warm colors are often used in eating areas, like breakfast or dining rooms.

Warm colors also help make north-facing rooms more inviting. Research has shown that people actually feel warmer in a room painted with yellows, reds, or oranges than they do in a white or blue room. In colder climates, warm colors are a popular choice.

Opposite: Warm colors range from intense yellows, reds, and oranges to more subtle salmons and browns. Warm colors are common choices for morning rooms or for active nighttime spaces.

Below: Shades of brown, ranging from caramel to burnt umber, warm up a decorating scheme.

22 TH 2 OVERSEA

22 TH 3 BOUT

VELY LIL

TH 4 LILA

22 TH

29 TH

BLOSSO

22 TH 4 LIN

28 TH 2 BLUE DRIFT (W)

28 TH 3 SCANDINAVIA (W)

28 TH 4 BRIGHT EYES (M)

28 TH 5 VAGRANT BLUE (M)

28 TH 6 DEEP NIGHT (D)

L-123

Cool Colors

*B*lues, greens, lavenders, and grays are cool colors. Intense cool colors are fresh and dramatic, while subdued cool grays are tranquil. Cool colors make rooms feel less confining. They are often used in bathrooms and other small rooms, as well as in bedrooms and formal living areas.

Use cool colors in west-facing kitchens, porches, and other areas where afternoon heat is a problem. In very warm climates, using whites and cool colors exclusively can make an entire house seem more comfortable.

Opposite: Cool colors range from bright violet, royal blue, and jade green to pale mint green and rich indigo blue. Cool colors are frequently used to create a relaxing atmosphere in bedrooms, bathrooms, and living rooms.

Below: Including cool blues in a decorating scheme gives the room a tranquil, calming tone.

S-123

27 TH 13

27 TH 15 CATALINA (W)

T-12

T-133

27 TH 16 ROBE BLUE (M)

(W)

(W)

27 TH 17 LIMPID (

27 TH 18 BLUE

S-123

S-131

L-130

15 TH 6 LUSTY YELLOW (D)

L-36

Bright Colors

*B*right colors are highly saturated with pigment. They are created by pure hues that are not diluted by white or darkened by black. Bright colors command attention and work well in active spaces, such as recreation rooms, sun porches, and children's rooms. In rooms that receive little natural light, such as a basement recreation room, painting the walls a bright color will help the room seem less dreary.

Because bright colors draw attention, they are often used as bold accents in rooms with a neutral or subdued color scheme. Balancing a single dominant bright color with neutral furnishings and elements creates another effective color scheme. Bright colors create a sense of excitement and energy and should be used with restraint in rooms intended for relaxing.

Opposite: A living room that balances bright-colored walls with neutral elements and furnishings creates a cheerful but simple atmosphere.

Below: Infusing a room with bright yellow and blue accents creates a vivid, exciting decorating scheme.

26 TH 21 BEACHFRONT BLUE (W)

12 TH 2 WHITE

4 TH 3 TYRIA

26 TH 22 BORN BLUE (M)

12 TH 3 PATINA (W

4 TH 4 MADON

S TH 23 BURNT BLUE

Subdued Colors

Subdued colors are less saturated with pigment than bright colors. These desaturated colors are created by adding a mixture of white, black, or gray to a pure hue. The greater the percentage of these added colors, the more neutral the base color becomes. Subdued colors are relaxing and restful, and are frequently used to create a tranquil mood in bedrooms, studies, and other quiet retreats. The quiet nature of subdued colors also makes them a popular choice for bathrooms and dressing rooms.

Subdued colors should be carefully balanced with neutral- or bright-colored features. Add interest to a room with a dominant subdued color by featuring a few brightly colored accents.

Opposite: Featuring walls painted with subdued colors, these living rooms have a restful, tranquil mood.

Below: Neutral-toned subdued colors, in shades of khaki, olive, and tan, add depth to a beige color scheme.

Building a Color Scheme

A new color scheme can dramatically change a room or your entire home. Even without changes of furniture or carpeting, a fresh infusion of color and pattern can transform the most ordinary room into an inviting living space.

Most room designs use one of three basic color schemes. A *single-color scheme,* also called a monochromatic scheme, uses one color in varying shades, such as light and dark blues. A *related color scheme,* sometimes called an analogous scheme, features two or three colors that are next to each other on the color wheel. A room decorated in blues and lavenders is an example of a related color scheme. A *complementary color scheme* uses colors that are opposite each other on the color wheel, like peach and blue.

Since color schemes are based on very personal choices, your rooms should feature color combinations you enjoy. But knowing exactly which colors to choose can be difficult. The following pages will help you select color schemes that suit your needs and tastes. In the following pages, you will discover how the color scheme affects the appearance of a room and the way it makes you feel. Knowing the effects of individual colors, which you learned in the last section, you will be able to apply the information in this section to combine colors in a way that serves the needs of a particular room.

Single-color Scheme

A single-color scheme uses varying shades of the same color. Single-color schemes are easy to develop, and lend a restful feeling to a room. These schemes offer much more variety than you might expect.

Varying the color values—including both light and dark values—and featuring some neutral-toned elements help keep a room interesting and balanced. The intensity of the colors you choose and the types of pattern work together to create effects that range from quietly subtle to outrageously dramatic. In addition to building a scheme around a pure color, you can use white or a neutral color, such as beige or gray, as the basis for a single-color scheme.

In general, the lighter elements in a single-color scheme tend to stand out the most. Highlight the most attractive features of the room with light colors, and use dark colors to downplay the less attractive features. In small homes, repeating a single color scheme with a variety of patterns and textures in adjoining rooms helps tie the rooms together.

Opposite: This subtle blue scheme features a delicate balance of pale blue variations, balanced with neutral cream-toned features.

Below: Varying shades of medium blue and dark blue accents create a scheme that allows the neutral-toned furnishings to stand out.

Related Color Scheme

Using varying shades of two or three colors located close together on the color wheel creates a related color scheme. For instance, a selection of blue, purple, and violet hues forms a harmonious related scheme, as does a combination of various yellows and greens. The values of the colors you feature will determine the overall feeling of the room. Related light colors will have a relaxing effect, while related dark colors will make the room seem more elegant and formal.

A room decorated with a related scheme has a unified, quiet feeling. Although this is a relatively easy scheme to create, the colors should be carefully balanced to avoid giving the room a one-dimensional appearance. To avoid creating a flat room, choose one or two dominant colors. Then, add accents to these colors, using hues that are farther away on the color wheel from the dominant colors. For example, if you are working with a lavender and blue related scheme, feature various shades of lavender and pale blue for some of the room's most dominant features, and select a few dark blue and purple accents. To give the scheme balance, use neutral shades, such as white, cream, or gray, in other dominant features.

Opposite: Purples, blues, and greens are present in this related scheme. The dark purple and green accents, as well as the strong neutral-toned elements, work together to balance the scheme.

Below: This blue and purple scheme is enlivened with dark blue, purple, and magenta accents.

Complementary Color Scheme

omplementary color schemes range from cheerful and vibrant to arresting and dramatic. These schemes are formed by using variations of colors located opposite one another on the color wheel, such as peach and pale blue, or pink and light green. In a successful complementary scheme, the colors play off of each other to bring out the best in the contrasting hues. A simple way to work with a complementary scheme is to choose one group of warm colors and another group of contrastingly cool colors. Complementary colors can be equally balanced, or one color can dominate the scheme to give the room an overall warm or cool tone.

As with a related color scheme, the hues comprising a complementary scheme must be carefully balanced and include some neutral-toned elements to soften the contrast in the complementary tones. Decide whether you want the room to have an overall light or dark tone, then choose accent colors opposite in tone. For example, a light complementary scheme is created by selecting pale complementary colors and light-colored neutrals for the dominant features and darker complementary accents.

Opposite: Peach and blue dominate the complementary scheme in a child's bedroom. The warm-toned wood dresser and striped rug add depth to the scheme.

Below: In this living room, warm peach is enhanced by cool blue accents.

Using Pattern

*P*atterns increase visual interest and texture in a decorating scheme. Although wallcoverings and upholstered furniture are the boldest ways to introduce pattern to a room, subtler pattern accents, such as window treatments, area rugs, and small throw pillows are also effective. A well-designed room may use only one pattern or many different patterns that are related by color or style.

The following pages illustrate how all patterns can be classified in one of four categories: geometric patterns, large patterns, small patterns, and overall patterns. Each pattern type can greatly influence a room's style. For example, a bold, abstract print wallcovering immediately establishes a contemporary style, while a wallcovering with a small floral design will suggest a more traditional or country theme.

Pattern works hand-in-hand with color scheme. As you read this section, pay attention to the ways in which the colors in a patterned wallcovering, carpet, or window treatment can enhance the overall color scheme of a room.

Like colors, patterns have an effect on the way you perceive a room. In this section, you'll see how patterns can create an illusion of height or space. You'll also learn about how the type of pattern affects a room's tone. Having an awareness of the visual effects and characteristics of each pattern type will help you achieve the look you want.

Geometric Patterns

Plaids, stripes, grids, and checks are some of the most common geometric patterns featured in decorating schemes. Large geometric patterns tend to be bold and exciting; when used as a dominant feature they have a stimulating effect. However, if used sparingly they add a touch of surprise and charm. Small geometric patterns leave a more subtle impression, quietly introducing accent colors into a room's color scheme. To prevent a room from looking too busy, balance dominant geometric patterns with solid-color accents.

Unlike other patterns, geometric patterns can emphasize a room's architectural attributes or downplay its flaws. When skillfully applied, a geometric pattern can create optical illusions. For instance, patterns with strong vertical lines can make a ceiling seem higher, and patterns with strong horizontal lines can help tall features appear shorter.

Opposite: The diagonal-check wallcovering and vertical striped panels draw the eye upward, adding height to the room.

Below: The strong grid pattern of the wallcovering emphasizes the shape of the room. The neutral-toned furniture and carpeting balance the pattern.

Large Patterns

*F*lorals, fruits, and vegetables are just a few of the designs commonly found on wallcoverings and fabrics with large patterns. In general, large patterns are stimulating and look best in an active area, such as a child's room, large kitchen, hallway, play room, or family room. Use large patterns sparingly in rooms typically used for relaxing, such as bedrooms and master bathrooms. When carefully chosen, a few large-patterned accents—such as an area rug, throw pillow, or small-scale window treatment—will add a spark of interest to a room's overall color scheme. In most cases, it's best to feature only one large pattern in a room. If there is more than one, the patterns lose their charm and the room looks too busy.

Like dark colors, large patterns seem to advance toward you, making rooms feel smaller and more cozy. A large-patterned wallcovering is a sure way to make a large, intimidating room feel more inviting. Large patterns may be included in the decorating scheme for a small room, but if they are featured too prominently, the room will feel crowded.

Opposite: Dark, large patterned walls appear to move toward you, creating an enveloping space.

Below: The large patterned wallcovering makes the living room seem smaller and more intimate.

Small Patterns

Small patterns add a touch of contrast to the background color scheme, quietly enhancing its effect. Like light colors, small patterns appear to recede, making close spaces seem larger and more open. For this reason, they are often used to create an illusion of space in small kitchens and bathrooms.

Small patterns have a tendency to "wash out," or lose their visual impact, when used over large wall or floor spaces. If you would like to use a small-patterned wallcovering or carpeting, balance the print with solids or with another pattern style. On walls, for instance, a coordinating large-patterned border can be used at crown molding or chair rail height to break up a small pattern. Similarly, a small area rug with a large or overall pattern can be used to balance small-print carpeting. It is often difficult to imagine how a small pattern will look when used over a large area, so try to get as large a sample as possible to take home. If you're considering a small patterned wallcovering, it is worth the expense to buy a whole roll to get an accurate idea of how it will look.

Opposite: The small pattern found in the wallcovering on the upper walls is balanced by large-pattern draperies and a wallcovering with an overall pattern on the lower walls.

Below: The small patterned wallcovering adds interest to a room dominated by neutral furnishings.

Overall Patterns

Perhaps the most engaging pattern of all, overall patterns seem to form a single, tight design. The colors appear to blend together, minimizing the pattern and emphasizing the color. Overall prints are extremely versatile and can be used in any room, either as a dominant element or as a subtle accent. Because overall patterns play tricks on the eye, it is wise to study the pattern—both up close and from a distance—before deciding on whether it will work with your decorating scheme.

If your decorating tastes are conservative or you're hesitant about working with patterns, an overall pattern is often a safe option for your decorating scheme. Using more than one overall pattern in a room adds texture and interest and quietly introduces accent colors that tie the scheme together. Overall patterns are also compatible with geometric, large, and small patterns in coordinating hues. They can be featured in the same room with one or more of these other types of patterns, provided the room is balanced with solid- and neutral-toned elements.

Opposite: The dominant overall patterned wallcovering is perfectly balanced with the large-patterned upholstered chair and framed prints.

Below: A soft wash of dark blue is created by this overall-patterned wallcovering.

Creating a Mood

*I*f you are having trouble deciding on a decorating scheme for a room, it may help to think about how you want to feel when you use the room. For instance, you may want a kitchen that makes you feel cheerful or a bedroom that puts you into a relaxed frame of mind.

Each color or combination of colors inspires a different feeling or mood. Once you have identified the tone for a room, all you need to do is select the corresponding hues. Patterns also have a strong effect on the mood of a room.

The following pages feature some popular themes for rooms and describe the types of colors used to invoke the mood. There are also suggestions on which types of rooms are suited for specific moods. The photographs illustrate these possibilities, giving you ideas for ways to create mood-inspired decorating schemes.

Bold Schemes

*B*old color schemes are created with high contrast tones, such as whites and blacks, and complementary hues. Hard-edged geometric patterns and dark walls also contribute to these striking designs. Bold schemes work especially well in entryways and foyers, and can also be appropriate in living rooms.

Subtle Schemes

Comfortable, subtle decorating schemes use subdued complementary colors. They often include a careful balance of warm- and cool-toned elements. Subtle schemes are always a safe choice—they are appropriate for any room in your home.

Cheerful Schemes

An airy, cheerful room is created by using light saturated colors that make the room seem larger. To maintain an open feeling, use low-contrast pastel furnishings and minimal window treatments for maximum sunlight. A cheerful scheme works well in any frequently used room, and children's rooms.

Tranquil Schemes

Using cool related colors that have low contrast is the key to creating a tranquil scheme. To unify the room, use coordinating patterns that repeat the color scheme in draperies, artwork, rugs, and other accents. Use a tranquil scheme in rooms that serve as relaxing retreats.

Formal Schemes

*F*ormal decorating schemes use dark accent colors, rich fabrics, and classically detailed patterns that draw attention. To create a more intimate atmosphere, choose a rich, dark color for the walls. Guest bedrooms, dining rooms, powder rooms, and parlors are all well-suited for a formal decorating scheme.

Natural Schemes

Warm earth tones with simple patterns and textures are the basis of natural schemes. Often, the warmth of brown tones is balanced with light cool colors, such as blue and gray. Libraries and family rooms often feature a natural scheme.

Finalizing a Room Design

*A*fter you have chosen a color scheme and a mood for a room, you are ready to select the paint, wallcovering, and fabrics to complete your decorating scheme. The information in this section will help you sort through and organize samples and show you how to make the best selections.

In this section, you will learn how to save time and simplify decisions by working with coordinated collections of fabrics, wallcoverings, and borders. Although they can cost more than other materials, coordinates are an easy way to create a professional-looking room.

project *Living Room*
purchase date *Sept. 29*
name/color *Volcano / Peach*
manufacturer *Christiansons*
other info *Matching boarders*
available (6-week
delivery - special order)
store *Stephanson Design*
salesperson *Michael Taylor*
price *32.⁵⁰/roll*

PAINT
project *Master Bedroom*
purchase date *June 23*
name/color *Cashmere White*
finish *Semi-Gloss*
quantity *3 Gallons*
manufacturer *Christian*
store *Warner's*
salesperson

This section also shows you how to work with existing elements, such as countertops, floor coverings, and plumbing fixtures, and how to incorporate them into the new decorating plan. You will also learn how to collect samples of your existing elements to take along when selecting paint, wallcovering, and other treatments.

Narrowing your selections down to a few samples at the decorating center can be a difficult task. On the following pages, you'll learn methods used by professional decorating consultants to narrow their choices, and how to select a handful of samples to take home for closer consideration.

You will also find some tried-and-true methods for testing samples in the rooms you plan to redecorate. These will help you get a realistic idea of how specific shades of paint, wallcoverings, and fabric will look when the decorating process is completed.

Coordinated Collections

Coordinated collections of fabrics, wallcoverings, and borders give you great flexibility in designing a room. By using the same fabric in draperies, pillows and furniture slipcovers, you can unify a room.

These collections offer more flexibility than you might imagine. Working with coordinates, you can create a low-contrast, high-contrast, or multi-pattern scheme in a room. Each of these schemes will have a different effect on the look and feel of a room.

Low-contrast Scheme

A single pattern in the fabric unifies the draperies and furniture. Here, the wall color was chosen to match the light background color in the fabric. This makes the room seem larger by helping the furniture blend into the walls. Repeating the same pattern will help unify adjoining rooms.

High-contrast Scheme

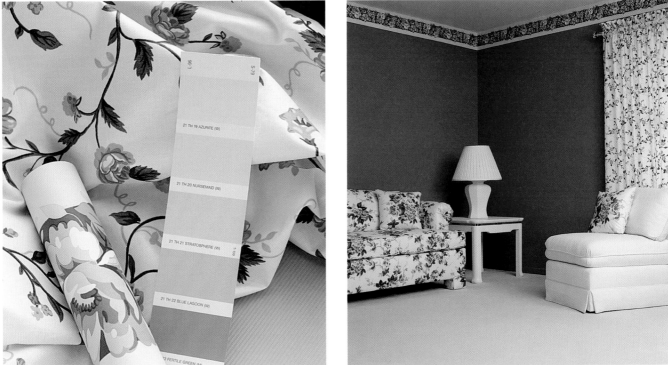

The dark green in the fabric is used as the background wall color to form a strong contrast with the light carpeting and upholstery fabrics. The detailed pattern in the wallcovering border contrasts with the solid colors surrounding it.

Multi-pattern Scheme

Several different patterns can be combined successfully in the same room. The different patterns in this room are unified by related floral designs and repeated colors. The wallcovering border helps blend the room elements together.

Working with Existing Colors

You may find it necessary to base the color scheme of a room on existing surfaces or fixtures that you are not replacing, such as tiles or carpet, or a colored tub, sink, or toilet. Countertops are other elements that are often retained because they are expensive to replace.

An easy way to blend these permanent fixtures into the new look of a room is by choosing paint colors and wallcovering that carry more visual weight than the old fixture.

If the existing surfaces are pastel or neutral, you can draw attention away from them by introducing stronger or brighter colors in the room. For example, if porcelain fixtures in a bathroom are mint green, you might select a patterned wallcovering that is predominately forest green. If the existing colors are bright, you can soften their impact with the addition of calm colors.

You can also mimic the existing colors in subtle features of a wallcovering or in small accessories, such as a soap dish or a telephone. This can make the old fixture or surface appear as a legitimate element of the decorating plan.

Tips for Working with Existing Colors

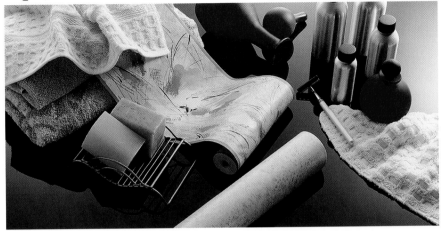

Bright fixtures (cobalt blue, in this bathroom) should be balanced with neutrals. To tie in the bold fixtures, add small accessories in the bright hue.

This color sample represents the existing bright blue porcelain fixtures.

Pastel fixtures, such as a light green tub, sink, and toilet, draw less attention when they are surrounded by brighter or darker shades of the same color. Shown here, darker greens have been used with light green fixtures. Yellow accessories are used as accents.

This color sample represents the existing green porcelain fixtures.

Gray floor tiles can be balanced by adding accessories in striking colors. Shown here, black, white, and red are used to accessorize a room, with touches of gray in the wallcovering.

This color sample represents the existing gray tiles.

Paint & Wallcovering Selection

When you begin shopping for a new paint color or wallcovering, bring fabric swatches and other samples of your home furnishings to the decorating center. Photographs of a room can give you and others a helpful perspective of the room's layout and architectural features.

Many decorating centers have professional design consultants who help customers at no charge. The paint selection display in a home decorating center can hold more than a thousand different colors, and wallcovering departments may have several hundred sample books. By comparing the samples from your home with the store's paint swatches and wallcovering samples, you can narrow your selections quickly.

Always bring several paint or wallcovering samples back to your home for a day or two before making a final selection. Look at the samples in the room you are decorating to see how the colors and patterns interact with the existing furnishings. Remember that colors change under different lighting conditions, so follow the 24-hour test on page 57.

Tips for Selecting Paint & Wallcovering

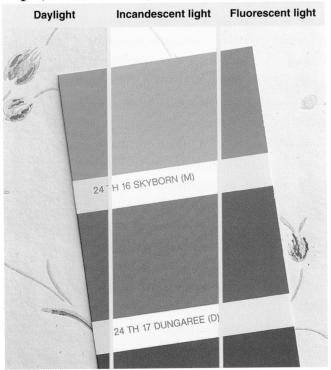

In the store, check paint chips and wallcovering samples in daylight as well as under artificial lighting. And remember that store lighting can differ from home lighting.

Take home no more than three different color and wallcovering samples. Fewer alternatives make the final decision easier.

Look at the dark end of a paint chip card to determine the tint base of an off-white paint. Almost all off-white hues contain a hint of another color.

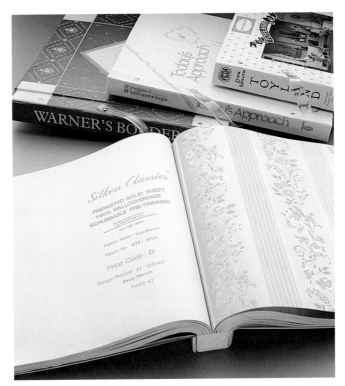

Choose wallcovering books by quickly flipping through them. A quick glance saves time and can tell you which books you will want to study more carefully.

(continued next page)

Tips for Selecting Paint & Wallcovering (continued)

Tape four paint chips together. Larger color samples are easier to judge. Cut off the white borders, which can be distracting.

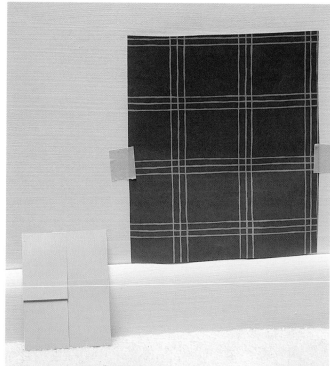

Judge samples of paint and wallcovering in the room where they will be used. Stand color samples upright to duplicate the way light strikes a wall surface. Tape wallcovering samples against the walls where they will be hung.

Before making a final decision, cut a large sample of wallcovering to use in the 24-hour test (page opposite). Decorating centers will usually provide large samples or let you borrow sample books.

Buy a quart of your chosen paint color. Paint a large sample card to hang on the wall. Follow the 24-hour test (page opposite) before buying the full amounts of paint and wallcovering needed.

The 24-Hour Test

Lighting affects color. To judge how paint or wall-covering will look in a specific area, hang a large sample on the wall and check it from time to time over the course of a full day. Notice how the color changes under varying lighting situations. If a room is most often used at a particular time of day, look at the color carefully at this time. Paint and wallcovering colors will look different in your home than they do in the decorating center. Furniture, woodwork, and floors reflect their own colors onto the walls, changing their appearance.

Incandescent indoor lighting generally has a yellow cast, although the choice of light bulb and shade can change its tint.

Natural daylight has a blue cast at midday, but has a warm orange tint at sunrise and sunset.

Basic Painting
& Wallcovering

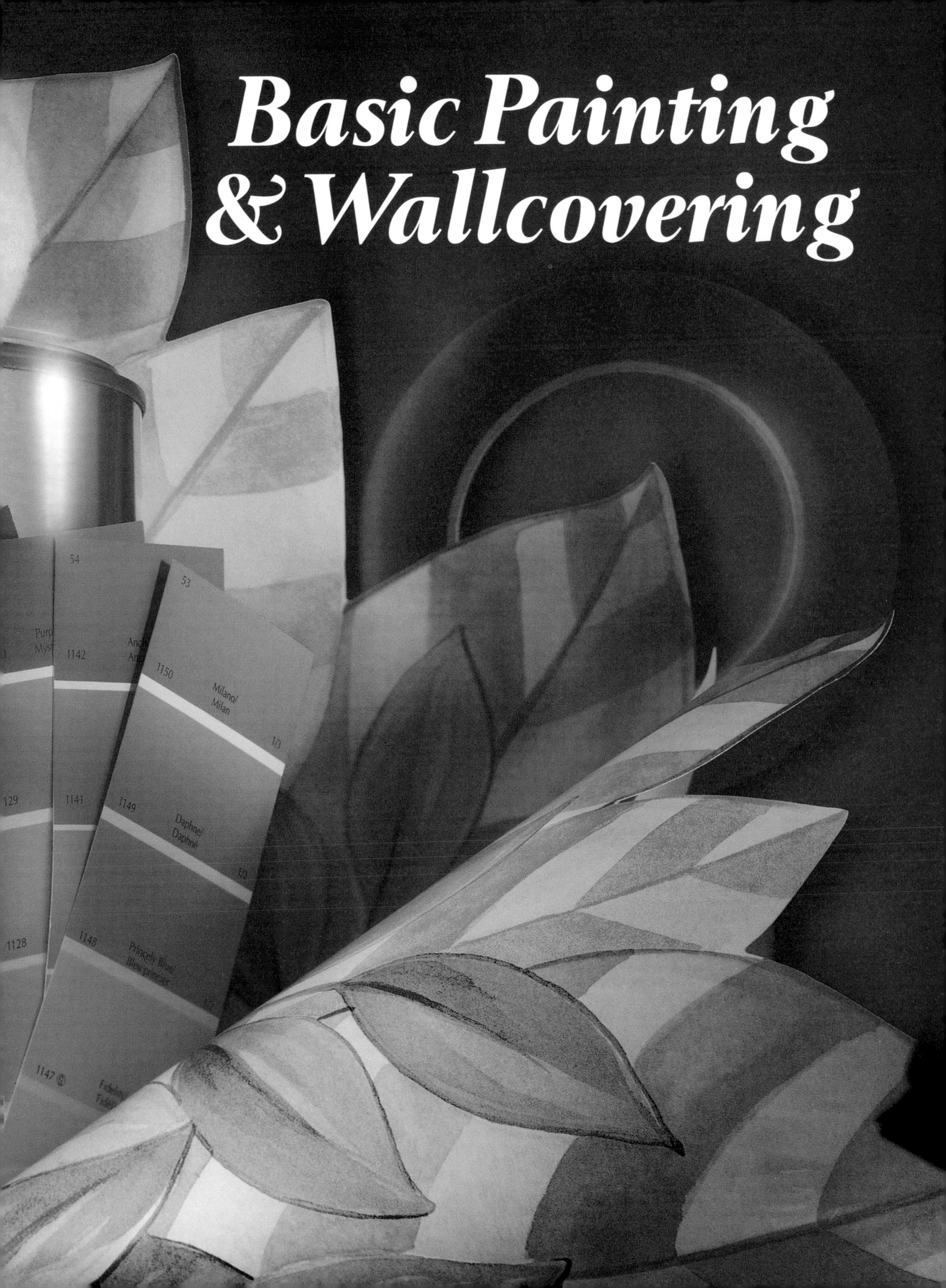

54

53

Purp
Myst

1142

1150

Milano/
Milan

1/3

129

1141

1149

Daphne/
Daphné

1/2

1128

1148

Princely Blue
Bleu prince

1147

Fichelien
Fidd

Making Preparations

*P*reparation is the key to ensuring the success of a painting or wallcovering project. The preparation process includes selecting the proper tools, removing or covering items that need protection, repairing walls and ceilings, repairing woodwork, masking and draping, and applying primers.

In this section, you will learn how to choose the tools and materials you'll need for preparation—the items favored by professional painters. You will also learn many time-saving "tricks of the trade" that will help you work more efficiently.

The guidelines outlined for preparing a room provide an easy-to-follow plan for protecting furniture, hardware, and fixtures from unwanted paint splatters.

Blemished walls must be given a new, smooth surface before they can accept paint or wallcovering.

Using the methods shown here for preparing and repairing walls and ceilings, you can effectively remove old wallcoverings, conceal stains, eliminate mildew, patch peeling paint, conceal surface imperfections, and repair holes. This section also includes tips for repairing woodwork before staining or painting.

Masking and draping can be the most time consuming part of the preparation process. Following the steps outlined in this section will simplify the task.

The final preparation step, priming or sealing, is critical to a quality finish. To ensure professional-quality results, follow the guidelines in this section to prime and seal all surfaces before painting or staining.

easy-mask PAINTING TAPE ⋅ DAUBERT ⋅ OAK BROOK, IL ⋅ USA   WET PA

OT TO BE APPLIED TO
FINISHES OR WALLPAPER
SURFACES THAT PEEL!

Ladders & Scaffolds

*T*wo quality stepladders and an extension plank are all you need to paint most interior surfaces. For painting high areas, build a simple scaffold by running the plank through the steps of two stepladders. It can be easy to lose your balance or step off the plank, so choose tall ladders for safety; the upper part of the ladders can help you balance and will keep you from stepping off the ends of the plank. Buy a strong, straight 2" × 10" board no more than 12 feet long, or rent a plank from a material dealer or rental outlet.

A manufacturer's sticker provides weight ratings and instructions for the correct use of the ladder. Read it carefully when shopping for a ladder. Choose a ladder that will easily accommodate your weight plus the additional weight of any tools or materials you plan to carry up the ladder.

How to Make a Scaffold

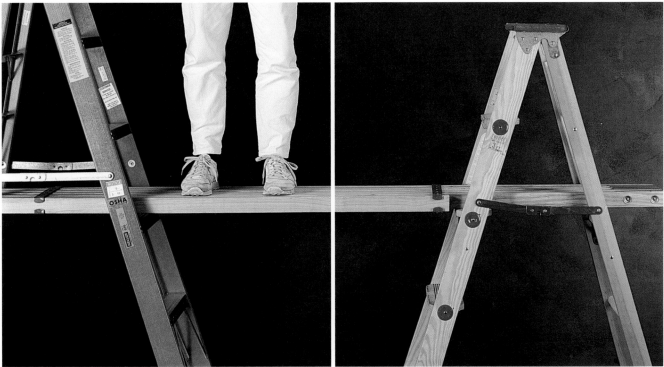

For ceilings and high spots on walls, make a simple scaffold by running an extension plank through the steps of two stepladders. The plank should be no more than 12 feet long. The ladders should face away from each other, so that the steps are on the inside of the scaffold. Make sure the ladder braces are down and locked, and watch your footing.

How to Use a Scaffold in Stairways

For stairs, run an extension plank through the step of a ladder, and place the other end on a stairway step. Make sure the ladder is steady, and check to see that the plank is level. Keep the plank close to the wall, if possible, and never overreach.

Tips for Using Ladders & Scaffolds

Rent extension planks from a paint dealer or from a rental center.

Choose straight planks without large knots or cracks. Choose 2" × 10" boards that have some spring in them: old, brittle wooden planks can break unexpectedly.

Push braces completely down and make certain they are locked. Legs of the ladder should be level and steady against the ground.

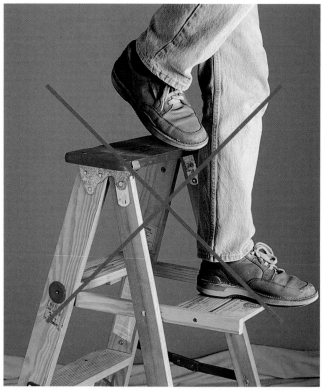

Do not stand on the top step, top brace, or on the utility shelf of a stepladder.

Center your weight on the ladder. Move the ladder often: do not overreach.

Keep steps tight by periodically checking them and tightening the braces when they need it.

Keep the ladder in front of you when working. Lean your body against the ladder for balance.

An adjustable ladder adapts to many different work needs. It can be used as a straight ladder, a stepladder, or as a base for scaffold planks.

Pressure sprayer

Pail

Work light

Sponge

Rubber gloves

Paintbrush

Cordless drill

Sanding block

Power sander

Heat gun

Wallboard knives

Putty knife

Flashlight

Wallcovering scorer

Preparation Tools & Materials

You can reduce or eliminate most cleanup chores by buying the right prep tools. For example, buy plastic or paper throwaway pails for mixing patching plaster, taping compound, or spackle. When the patcher hardens in the container, just throw it away: You'll avoid the job of washing out the pail and also avoid clogging plumbing drains with plaster.

Use a sponge or wallboard wet sander to smooth plaster or wallboard compound while it is still soft, rather than waiting until it dries and becomes difficult to sand.

Buy a variety of patching tools. You will need a narrow putty knife for reaching into small spaces. Purchase a wide knife or trowel for patching holes in walls or ceilings. A wide tool that overlaps both edges of a hole will help you patch with fewer passes of the tool, reducing trowel marks and minimizing the need for sanding.

Masking and draping materials: plastic and canvas drop cloths, masking papers, masking tape dispenser, masking tape, and painter's tape.

Removal agents help prepare surfaces for paint and wallcovering, and speed cleanup. Clockwise from top left are: wallpaper dough, cleanup solution, wallcovering remover, and trisodium phosphate (TSP).

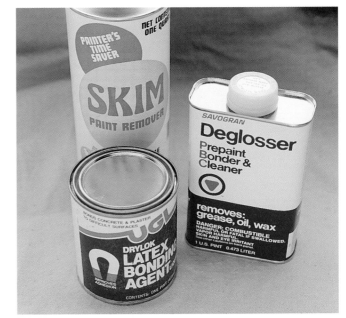

Preparation liquids include (clockwise from top left): paint remover; liquid deglosser, for dulling glossy surfaces prior to painting; and latex bonding agent, for plaster repairs.

Primer and sealers provide a good base coat that bonds with paint or a varnish finish. From left to right are: sanding sealer, PVA primer, shellac, and alkyd wallboard primer.

Other materials include: cleaning and patching compounds (A), repair patch (B), fiberglass joint tape (C), sink and tub caulk (D), replacement tiles (E), wall hangers (F), and sandpaper (G).

Room Preparation

How to Prepare a Room

Before painting, your first step is to protect everything that could be covered by dust or splattered by paint. Remove all window and door hardware, light fixtures, and the coverplates on outlets and wall switches. Drape furniture and cover the floors. Remove heating and air conditioning duct covers. Mask off wood moldings with self-adhesive paper or masking tape.

Tip:

When removing hardware, mark the pieces with masking tape for identification so that they can easily be replaced.

1 Remove all hardware, such as window handles and cabinet catches, from surfaces to be painted. If you will be installing new hardware, buy it now and drill new screw holes if needed.

2 Remove all nails, screws, and picture hangers from surfaces to be painted. To prevent damage to the plaster or wall-board, use a block of wood under the head of the hammer.

3 Remove covers from heating and air-conditioning ducts to protect them from splatters. Remove thermostats, or use masking tape to protect them against paint drips.

4 Move furniture to the center of the room and cover it with plastic sheets. In large rooms, leave an alley through the center for access if you are painting the ceiling. Cover floors with 9-ounce canvas drop cloths. Canvas absorbs paint spills.

5 Turn off the electricity. Remove the coverplates from outlets and switches, then replace the cover screws. Lower light fixtures away from electrical boxes, or remove the fixtures. Cover hanging fixtures with plastic bags.

Wallcovering Removal

Newer vinyl wallcoverings often can be peeled off by hand. Some will leave a paper and adhesive residue that is easily removed with water. With nonpeelable wallcoverings, pierce the surface with a perforation tool, then apply a remover solution to dissolve the adhesive.

Wallcovering remover fluids contain wetting agents that penetrate the paper and help soften the adhesive. Use a remover solution to wash away old adhesive after wallcovering is removed.

If the old wallcovering was hung over unsealed wallboard, it may be impossible to remove it without destroying the wallboard. You may be able to paint or hang new wallcovering directly over the old wallcovering, but the surface should be smooth and primed. Before painting over wallcovering, prime with alkyd wallboard primer.

How to Remove Wallcovering

1 If the wallcovering does not strip by hand, cover the floor with layers of newspaper. Add wallcovering remover fluid to a bucket of water, as directed by the manufacturer.

Find a loose edge and try to strip off the wallcovering. Vinyls often peel away easily.

2 Pierce the wallcovering surface with a perforation tool. This allows the remover solution to enter and soften the adhesive.

3 Use a pressure sprayer, paint roller, or sponge to apply the remover solution. Let it soak into the covering, according to the manufacturer's directions.

4 Peel away loosened wallcovering with a 6" wallboard knife. Be careful not to damage the plaster or wallboard. Remove all backing paper.

5 Rinse adhesive residue from the wall with remover solution. Rinse with clear water and let the walls dry completely.

Ceiling & Wall Repairs

*T*horoughly washing, rinsing, and sanding your walls before priming them will guarantee a long-lasting finish. For a professional appearance, carefully check your walls for damage and repair the wallboard or plaster as needed. Pregummed fiberglass wallboard tapes and premixed patching compounds reduce drying time and let you patch and paint a wall the same day.

Wash and sand before repainting. Use a TSP (trisodium phosphate) solution and a sponge to cut grease and to remove dirt. Wear rubber gloves, and wash walls from the bottom up, using a damp sponge, to avoid streaks. Rinse thoroughly with clean water. After drying, lightly sand surfaces.

How to Remove Stains

1 Apply stain remover to a clean, dry cloth, and rub lightly to remove the stain.

2 Seal all stain areas with white pigmented shellac. Pigmented shellac prevents stains from bleeding through the new paint.

3 Water or rust stains may indicate water damage. Check for leaking pipes and soft plaster, make needed repairs, then seal the area with stain-killing sealer.

How to Remove Mildew

1 Test stains by washing with water and detergent. Mildew stains will not wash out.

2 Wearing rubber gloves and eye protection, wash the walls with bleach, which kills mildew spores.

3 After the bleach treatment, wash away mildew with a TSP solution, and rinse with clear water.

How to Patch Peeling Paint

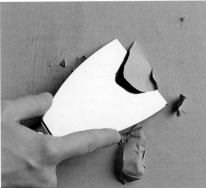

1 Scrape away loose paint with a putty knife or paint scraper.

2 Apply spackle to the edges of chipped paint with a putty knife or flexible wallboard knife.

3 Sand the patch area with 150-grit production sandpaper. The patch area should feel smooth to the touch.

How to Fill Nail Holes

1 Apply lightweight spackle to holes with a putty knife or your fingertip. This keeps repair areas small, so they are easy to hide with paint. Let the spackle dry.

2 Lightly sand the repair area with 150-grit production sandpaper. Production paper has an open surface that does not clog easily. Wipe away dust with a damp sponge, then prime the spot with PVA primer.

How to Fill Shallow Dents & Holes

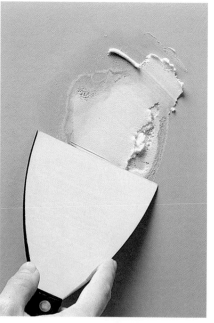

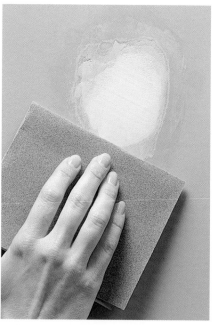

1 Scrape or sand away any loose plaster, peeled paint, or wallboard face paper to ensure a solid base for patching.

2 Fill the hole with lightweight spackle. Apply the spackle with the smallest wallboard knife that will span the entire hole. Let the spackle dry.

3 Lightly sand the area with 150-grit production sandpaper.

How to Fix Popped Wallboard Nails

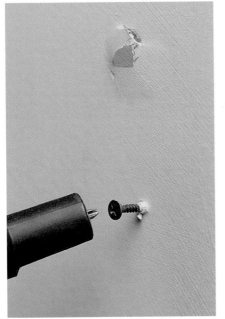

1 Drive a wallboard screw 2" away from popped nail. Be sure the screw hits a stud or joist and pulls the wallboard tight against the framing.

2 Scrape away loose paint or wallboard compound. Drive the popped nail back into the framing so the head is sunk ¹⁄₁₆" below the surface of the wallboard. Do not set the nail with a punch.

3 Use a wallboard knife to apply 3 coats of premixed wallboard compound to the nail and screw holes, letting it dry between coats. Sand and prime the patched area.

How to Repair Cracks in Plaster

1 Scrape away any texture or loose plaster around the crack. Reinforce the crack with pregummed fiberglass wallboard tape.

2 Use a taping knife or trowel to apply spackle or wallboard compound to cover over the tape so the tape is just concealed: if compound is too thick, it will recrack.

3 Apply a second thin coat if necessary to conceal the tape edges. Sand lightly and prime the repair area. Retexture the surface (pages 112–113).

How to Patch Small Holes in Wallboard

1 Inspect the damaged area. If there are no cracks around the edge of the hole, just fill the hole with spackle, let it dry, and sand the area smooth.

2 If the edges are cracked, cover the hole with a peel-and-stick repair patch. The patch has a metal mesh center for strength, and can be cut or shaped as needed. Patches are available in several sizes.

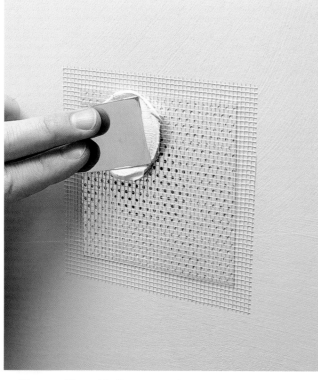

3 Use a wallboard knife to cover the patch with spackle or wallboard compound. Two coats may be needed. Let the patch set until it is nearly dry.

4 Use a damp sponge or wallboard wet sander to smooth the repair area. This eliminates dust caused by dry sanding.

How to Patch Larger Holes in Wallboard

1 Outline the damaged area with a framing square. Use a wallboard saw or jig saw to cut away the damaged section.

2 Install wood or wallboard backer strips. For wood, use a wallboard screw gun and 1¼" wallboard screws to secure the strip in place.

Or, use wallboard backers secured by hot glue as an alternative to wood backer strips. Cut a wallboard patch to size, then screw or glue the wallboard patch in place over the backer strips.

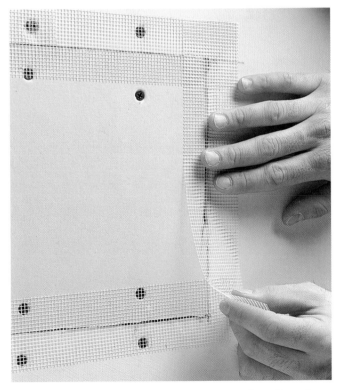

3 Apply wallboard tape to the cracks, then apply wallboard compound and wet-sand the area (page opposite).

Repairing Holes in Plaster

Modern repair methods and materials have simplified the job of repairing holes in plaster. Coating the patch area with latex bonding liquid ensures a good bond and a tight, crack-free patch. Bonding liquid also eliminates the need to wet the plaster and lath to prevent premature drying and shrinkage. Ask your hardware dealer for a good concrete/plaster latex bonding liquid.

How to Repair Holes in Plaster

1 Sand or scrape any textured paint from the area around the hole.

2 Test with a scraper to be sure the plaster is solid and tight around the damaged area. Scrape away any loose or soft plaster.

3 Apply latex bonding liquid liberally around the edges of the hole and over the base lath to ensure a crack-free bond between the old and new plaster.

4 Mix patching plaster as directed by the manufacturer, and use a wallboard knife or trowel to apply it to the hole. Fill shallow holes with a single coat of plaster.

5 For deeper holes, apply a shallow first coat, then scratch a crosshatch pattern in the wet plaster. Let it dry, then apply second coat of plaster. Let the plaster dry, and sand it lightly.

6 Use texture paint or wallboard compound to recreate any surface texture, as directed on pages 112–113.

Paint Removal for Wood

How to Use Chemical Stripper

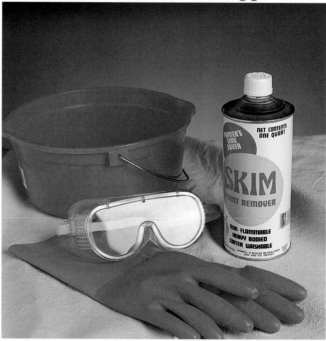

Follow label directions for the safe use of chemicals. Wear heavy rubber gloves and eye protection, use drop cloths, and open windows and doors for ventilation when working with chemical strippers.

*B*efore painting or refinishing, wood should be cleaned, repaired, and sanded. If the old paint is heavily layered or badly chipped, it should be stripped before the wood is repainted.

If you are using a heat gun to strip wood, take care not to scorch the wood. Never use a heat gun after using chemical strippers: the chemical residue may be vaporized or ignited by the heat.

When using a chemical paint stripper, always wear protective clothing and safety gear, including eye protection and a respirator. Follow the label directions for safe use, and always work in a well-ventilated area.

2 Apply a liberal coat of stripper to painted wood with a paint brush or steel wool. Let it stand until the paint begins to blister. Do not let the stripper dry out on wood surfaces.

3 Scrape away the paint with a putty knife or scraper and steel wool as soon as it softens. Rub the stripped wood with denatured alcohol and new steel wool to help clean the grain. Wipe the wood with a wet sponge or solvent, as directed on the stripper label.

How to Use a Heat Gun

1 Hold the heat gun near the wood until the paint softens and just begins to blister. Overheating can make the paint gummy and may scorch the wood. Always be careful when using a heat gun around flammable materials.

2 Remove softened paint with a scraper or putty knife. Scrapers are available in many shapes for removing paint from shaped moldings. Sand away any paint residue remaining after heat stripping.

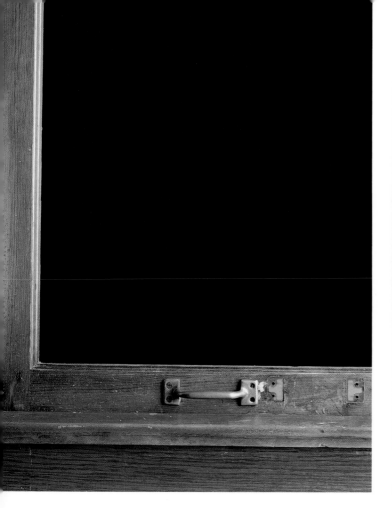

How to Prepare for Painting

1 Wash woodwork with TSP solution, and rinse. Scrape away any peeling or loose paint. Badly chipped woodwork should be stripped (pages 80–81).

How to Prepare for Refinishing

1 Clean woodwork with a soft cloth and odorless mineral spirits or liquid furniture refinisher.

Woodwork Patching

For the best results, woodwork should be cleaned, patched and sanded before it is re-painted. A liquid deglosser helps to dull shiny sur-faces so they will bond with new paint. If new hardware is to be installed, check to see if new pieces will fit old screw holes. If new screw holes must be drilled, fill the old holes with wood patcher.

To renew varnished wood, clean the surfaces with mineral spirits or furniture refinisher, then patch any holes with a wood patcher that is tinted to match the existing finish. Sand the wood smooth, and apply one or two coats of varnish.

2 Use a putty knife to apply latex wood patch or spackle to any nail holes, dents, and to any other damaged areas.

3 Sand the surfaces with 150-grit production paper until they are smooth to the touch. Wipe woodwork with a tack cloth before priming and painting.

2 Apply wood patch to holes and dents with a putty knife. Sand patch areas lightly with 150-grit production sandpaper.

3 Apply a clear wood sealer to the patch area (page 89). Restain the area to match the surrounding wood. Apply 1 or 2 coats of varnish.

Masking & Draping

For fast, mess-free painting, shield any surfaces that could get splattered. If you are painting only the ceiling, drape the walls and woodwork to prevent splatters. When painting walls, mask the baseboards and window and door casings.

Remove lightweight furniture, and move heavier pieces to the center of the room and cover them with plastic. Cover the floors with 9-ounce canvas drop cloths that will absorb paint splatters.

Masking and draping materials include (clockwise from top left): plastic and canvas drop cloths, self-adhesive plastic, masking tape, and pregummed masking papers. Plastic-paper laminates are also available.

How to Drape Walls

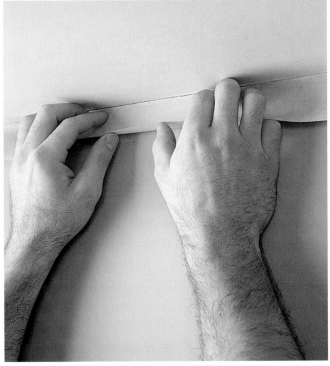

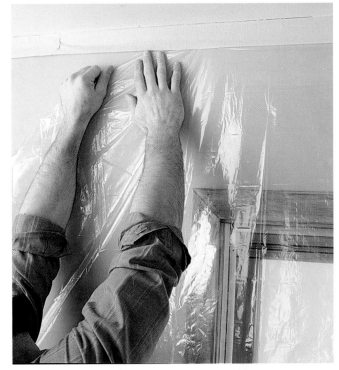

1 Press the top half of 2" masking tape along the joint between the ceiling and the wall. Leave the bottom half of the masking tape loose.

2 Hang sheet plastic under masking tape, draping the walls and baseboards. After painting, remove the loose edge as soon as the paint is too dry to run.

How to Mask Wood Trim

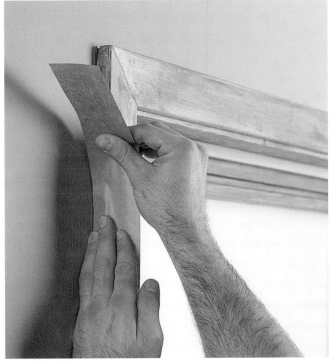

1 Use pregummed paper or wide masking tape to protect wood moldings from paint splatters. Leave the outside edge of masking tape loose.

2 After applying the tape, run the tip of a putty knife along the inside edge of the tape to seal against seeping paint. After painting, remove the tape as soon as the paint is too dry to run.

Final Check & Cleanup

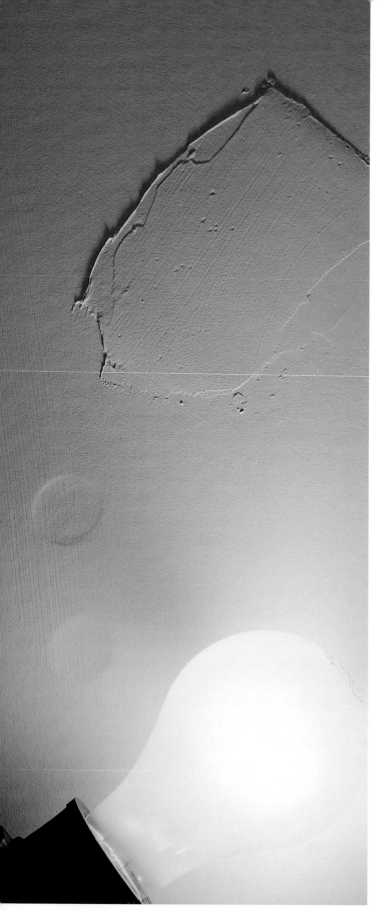

Before painting, make a final check of the work area. Clean the room thoroughly to eliminate dust that might collect on tools and settle on wet paint. Maintain the temperature and humidity levels recommended by product labels. This will help keep paint edges wet while painting, minimizing lap marks in the finished job.

It is also important for the paint to dry within normal time limits so dirt can't settle on the finish while it is wet. When applying wallcovering, a proper work climate prevents the adhesive from drying prematurely, which can cause blisters or loose edges on the wallcovering.

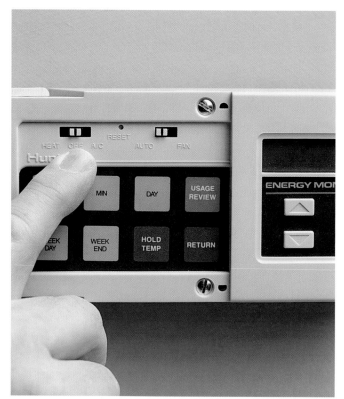

Check all surfaces to be painted with a strong sidelight. Sand, or spackle and sand, any rough spots that were missed in preparation.

Turn off thermostats for forced air furnaces and air conditioners so that the fan will not circulate dust through the area being painted.

Sand all surfaces that will be painted with 150-grit production sandpaper. Sanding dulls the surface so it will accept new paint. Wipe walls with a tack rag.

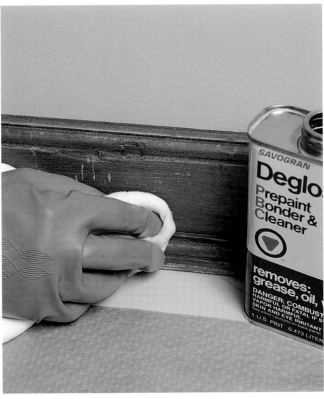

Wipe dust from woodwork with a tack rag, or with a clean cloth moistened with liquid deglosser.

Use a vacuum cleaner to pick up the dust from windowsills and window tracks, and from baseboards and casements.

If humidity levels are low, place a humidifier in the room before painting or wallcovering. This keeps paint or adhesive from drying too fast.

Primers & Sealers

A sealer should be applied to wood surfaces before they are varnished. Wood often has both hard and soft grains, as well as a highly absorbent end grain. Applying a sealer helps close the wood surface so that varnish is absorbed evenly in different types of wood grain. If the wood is not sealed, the varnish may dry to a mottled finish.

Primers are used to seal surfaces that will be painted. Wallboard seams and patch areas that have been treated with wallboard compound or patching material can absorb paint at a different rate than the surrounding areas. Joints and patch areas often show or "shadow" through the finished paint if the walls were not adequately primed.

Tint primer with color base available at paint dealers, or request that your dealer tint the primer. A color-matched primer provides an excellent base for the finish coat of paint.

Tips for Priming & Sealing

Seal raw wood by applying a primer before painting or a clear sealer before varnishing. Unsealed wood can produce a spotty finish.

Roughen gloss surfaces with fine sandpaper, then prime them to provide good bonding between the new and the old paint. Primers provide "tooth" for the new coat of paint.

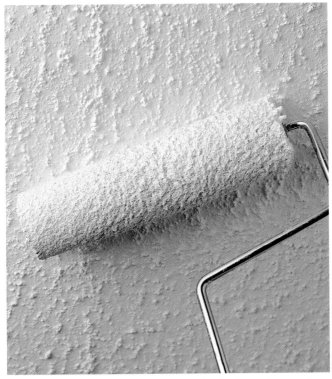

Seal textured surfaces with a PVA or alkyd primer, then apply a finish coat with a long-nap roller. Textured walls and ceilings soak up a lot of paint and make it difficult to apply paint evenly.

Spot-prime minor repair areas on plaster or wallboard with PVA primer.

Painting Techniques

A fresh coat of paint gives interior rooms new life. After the walls, ceilings, and woodwork have been cleaned, repaired, and prepared, an application of paint will hide the last traces of former blemishes, giving the room a dramatically improved appearance. Following the basic methods presented in this section will ensure that your painting projects have a professional-quality finish.

This section begins with all the information you need to safely work with, dispose of, and store painting materials. Following these guidelines will protect you and your family from harm, and ensure that you meet your community's environmental restrictions.

Choosing the right paint and tools for the job can be difficult, especially since there are so many choices available at paint suppliers and home centers. This section will provide you with a primer for selecting the right paint and tools for interior projects.

Using professional painting techniques eliminates errors, allows you to work more efficiently, and gives surfaces a flawless finish. The step-by-step instructions in this section explain the correct methods for using paintbrushes and rollers to paint trim and apply paint to walls and ceilings. From keeping a "wet edge" to texture painting, you will learn the techniques used by professional painters.

A paint project is not completed until the room and all of the tools have been cleaned. The tips at the end of this section will show you how to clean and store your painting tools, as well as how to remove the inevitable paint splatter.

Paint Safety

Always read and follow the label information on paint and solvent containers. Chemicals that pose a fire hazard are listed (in order of flammability) as: combustible, flammable, or extremely flammable. Use caution when using these products, and remember that the fumes are also flammable.

The warning "use with adequate ventilation" means that there should be no more vapor buildup than there would be if you were using the material outside. Open doors and windows, use exhaust fans, and wear an approved safety mask if you can smell paint or solvent.

Paint chemicals do not store well. Buy just as much as is needed for the project and keep chemicals away from children. Use up excess paint by applying an extra coat or follow local guidelines regarding paint disposal.

Read label information. Chemicals that are poisonous or flammable are labeled with warnings and instructions for safe handling.

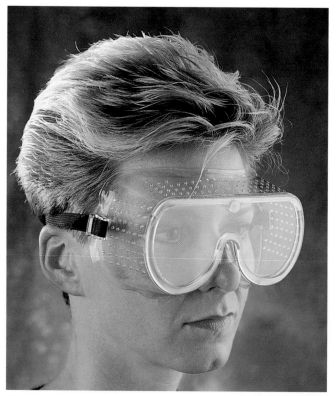

Wear safety goggles when using chemical stripper or cleaning products. Use goggles when painting overhead.

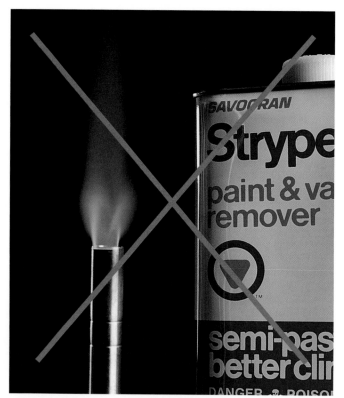

Do not use chemicals that are listed as combustible or flammable, such as paint strippers, near an open flame. Appliance pilot lights can ignite chemical vapors.

Open windows and doors and use a fan for ventilation when painting indoors. If a product label has the warning "harmful or fatal if swallowed," assume that the vapors are dangerous to breathe.

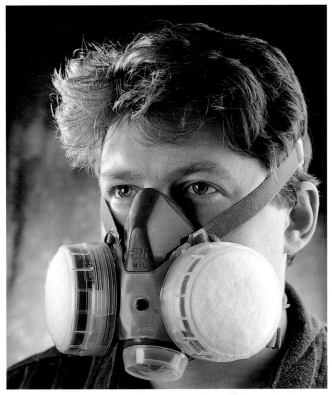

Use an approved mask to filter vapors if you cannot ventilate a work area properly. If you can smell vapors, the ventilation is not adequate.

Let thinners stand after cleaning your tools. When the solid material settles out, pour off the clear thinner and save it for reuse. Discard the sediment.

Dispose of leftover paint safely. Let the container stand uncovered until the solvent evaporates, then re-cover and dispose of the container with other trash.

Paint Selection

*P*aints are either water-base (latex) or alkyd-base. Latex paint is easy to apply and clean up, and the improved chemistry of today's latexes makes them suitable for nearly every application. Some painters feel that alkyd paint allows for a smoother finished surface, but local regulations may restrict the use of alkyd-base products.

Paints come in various sheens. Paint finishes range from flat to high-gloss enamels. Gloss enamels dry to a shiny finish, and are used for surfaces that need to be washed often, like walls in bathrooms and kitchens, and woodwork. Flat paints are used for most wall and ceiling applications.

Paint prices typically are an accurate reflection of quality. As a general rule, buy the best paint your budget can afford. High-quality paints are easier to use and they look better than cheaper paints. And because quality paints last longer and cover better than budget paints, often requiring fewer coats, they are usually less expensive in the long run.

Always use a good primer to coat surfaces before painting. The primer bonds well to all surfaces, and provides a durable base that keeps the finish coat from cracking or peeling. To avoid the need for additional coats of expensive finish paint, tint the primer to match the new color.

How to Estimate Paint

1) Length of wall or ceiling (feet)	
2) Height of wall, or width of ceiling	×
3) Surface area	=
4) Coverage per gallon of chosen paint	÷
5) Gallons of paint needed	=

How to Select a Quality Paint

Paint coverage (listed on can labels) of quality paint should be about 400 square feet per gallon. Bargain paints (left) may require two or even three coats to cover the same area as quality paints.

High washability is a feature of quality paint. The pigments in bargain paints (right) may "chalk" and wash away with mild scrubbing.

Paint Sheens

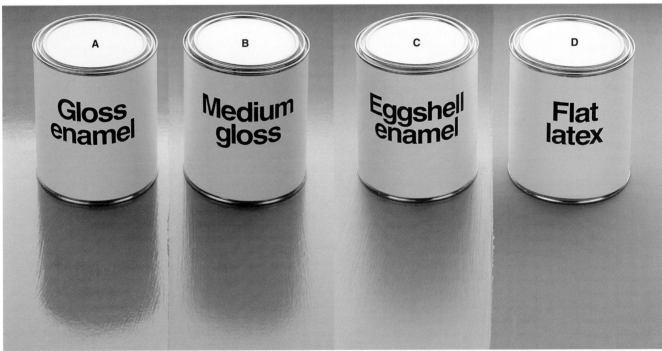

Paint comes in a variety of surface finishes, or sheens. Gloss enamel **(A)** provides a highly reflective finish for areas where high washability is important. All gloss paints tend to show surface flaws. Alkyd-base enamels have the highest gloss. Medium-gloss latex enamel creates a highly washable surface with a slightly less reflective finish. Like gloss enamels, medium-gloss paints **(B)** tend to show surface flaws. Eggshell enamel **(C)** combines the soft finish with the washability of enamel. Flat latex **(D)** is an all-purpose paint with a soft finish that hides surface irregularities.

Tools & Equipment

Most painting jobs can be done with a few quality tools. Purchase two or three premium brushes, a sturdy paint pan that can be attached to a stepladder, and one or two good rollers. With proper cleanup, these tools will last for years.

Brushes made of hog or ox bristles should be used only with alkyd-base paints. All-purpose brushes blend polyester, nylon, and sometimes animal bristles. Choose a straight-edged 3" wall brush, a 2" straight-edged trim brush, and a tapered sash brush.

How to Choose a Paintbrush

Chiseled end

Flagged bristles

Spacer plugs

Reinforced ferrule

Hardwood handle

A quality brush (left), has a shaped hardwood handle and a sturdy reinforced ferrule made of noncorrosive metal. Multiple spacer plugs separate the bristles. A quality brush has flagged (split) bristles and a chiseled end for precise edging. A cheaper brush (right) will have a blunt end, unflagged bristles, and a cardboard spacer plug that may soften when wet.

A 3" straight-edged brush (top) is a good choice for cutting paint lines at ceilings and in corners. For painting woodwork, a 2" trim brush (middle) works well. Choose brushes with chiseled tips for painting in corners. A tapered sash brush (bottom) can help when painting corners on window sashes.

Paint Rollers & Roller Accessories

A good paint roller is an inexpensive, timesaving tool that can last for years. Choose a standard 9" roller with a wire frame and nylon bearings. The roller should feel well balanced, and should have a handle molded to fit your hand. The handle should also have a threaded end that lets you attach an extension handle for painting ceilings and high walls.

Roller covers are available in a wide variety of nap lengths, but most jobs can be done with ⅜" nap. Select medium-priced synthetic roller covers that can be reused a few times before discarding. Bargain roller covers might shed fibers onto the painted surface, and cannot be cleaned and reused. Rinse all roller covers in solvent to prevent lint.

Use more expensive lamb's wool roller covers when using most alkyd-base paints. Mohair covers work well with gloss alkyd paints where complete smoothness is important.

Select the proper roller cover for the surface you intend to paint. A ¼"-nap cover (top) is used for very flat surfaces. A ⅜"-nap cover (middle) will cover the small flaws found in most flat walls and ceilings. A 1"-nap cover (bottom) fills spaces in rough surfaces, like concrete blocks or stucco walls.

Synthetic covers (left) are good with most paints, especially latexes. Wool or mohair roller covers (right) give an even finish with alkyd products. Choose good quality roller covers, which will be less likely to shed lint.

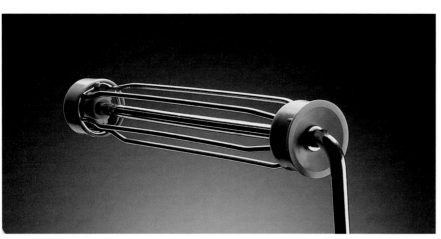

Choose a sturdy roller with a wire cage construction. Nylon bearings should roll smoothly and easily when you spin the cage. The handle end should be threaded for attaching an extension handle.

Buy a paint tray with legs that allow the tray to sit steadily on the shelf of a stepladder. A good paint tray will resist flexing when it is twisted. Look for a textured ramp that keeps the roller turning easily.

A five-gallon paint container and paint screen speed up painting of large areas. Load the paint roller straight from bucket, using a roller extension handle. Do not try to balance a paint pail on a stepladder shelf.

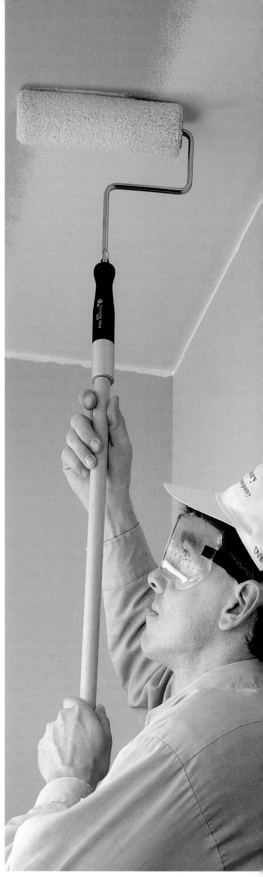

Use a 4-ft. extension handle to paint ceilings and walls easily without a ladder.

Specialty Painting Tools

An airless paint sprayer is useful for painting large areas or for irregular surfaces, like louvered closet doors. All sprayers produce some overspray, so wear protective gear and mask off all areas likely to be splattered. Movable workpieces should be painted outside or in your basement or garage. Thinning the paint before spraying will result in easier use of the tool and more even coverage.

Surfaces with unusual angles and contours are sometimes difficult to paint with standard rollers and brushes. Specialty tools make some painting situations easier. Disposable foam brushes, for instance, are excellent for applying an even coat of clear varnish to smooth woodwork, and paint gloves make painting contoured surfaces a much simpler task.

Specialty roller covers, available in a variety of light and heavy textures, make it easy to achieve a consistent, textured surface.

A bendable tool can be shaped to fit unusual surfaces, such as window shutters or the fins of cast-iron radiators.

A paint glove simplifies painting of pipes and other contoured surfaces, like wrought-iron.

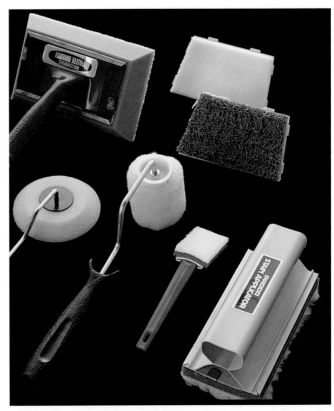

Paint pads and specialty rollers come in a wide range of sizes and shapes to fit different painting needs.

Aerosol spray paint speeds the painting of any small, intricate jobs, like heat registers.

A paint mixer bit attaches to a power drill to stir paints quickly and easily. Use a variable-speed drill at low speed to avoid air bubbles in the paint.

Mix paint together (called "boxing") in a large pail to eliminate slight color variations between cans. Stir the paint thoroughly with a wooden stick or power drill attachment. To keep paint from building up in the groove around the paint can lid, pound several small nail holes into the groove. This allows the paint to drip back into the can.

Basic Painting Methods

For a professional-looking paint job, spread the paint evenly onto the work surface without letting it run, drip, or lap onto other areas. Excess paint will run on the surface and can drip onto woodwork and floors. Stretching paint too far leaves lap marks and results in patchy coverage.

Start each section by "cutting in," with a brush on all edges, corners, and trim. Painting flat surfaces with brushes and rollers is a three-step process. First, apply the paint to the work surface, then distribute it evenly. Finally, smooth it out for a seamless finish.

How to Use a Paint Brush

1 Dip the brush, loading one-third of its bristle length. Tap the bristles against the side of the can. Dipping deeper over-loads the brush. Dragging the brush against the lip of the can causes the bristles to wear.

2 Cut in the edges using the narrow edge of the brush, press-ing just enough to flex the bristles. Keep an eye on the paint edge, and paint with long, slow strokes. Always paint from a dry area back into wet paint to avoid lap marks.

3 Brush wall corners using the wide edge of the brush. Paint open areas with a brush or roller before the brushed paint dries.

4 To paint large areas with a brush, apply the paint with 2 or 3 diagonal strokes. Hold the brush at a 45° angle to the work surface, pressing just enough to flex the bristles. Distribute the paint evenly with horizontal strokes.

5 Smooth the surface by drawing the brush vertically from the top to the bottom of the painted area. Use light strokes and lift the brush from the sur-face at the end of each stroke. This method is best for slow-drying alkyd enamels.

Painting Techniques 103

Roller Techniques

*P*aint surfaces in small sections, working from dry surfaces back into wet paint to avoid roller marks. If a paint job takes more than a day, cover the roller tightly with plastic wrap or store it in a bucket of water overnight to prevent the paint from drying out.

Wet the roller cover with water (when painting with latex paint) or mineral spirits (when painting with alkyd enamel), to remove lint and prime the roller cover. Squeeze out excess liquid. Fill the paint tray reservoir. Dip the roller fully into

How to Paint With a Paint Roller

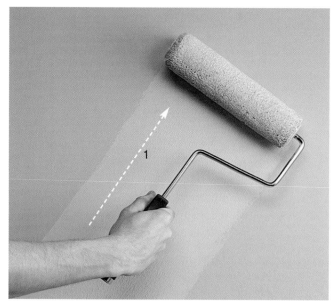

1 With the loaded roller, make a diagonal sweep (1) about 4' long on the surface. On walls, roll upward on the first stroke to avoid spilling paint. Use slow roller strokes to avoid splattering.

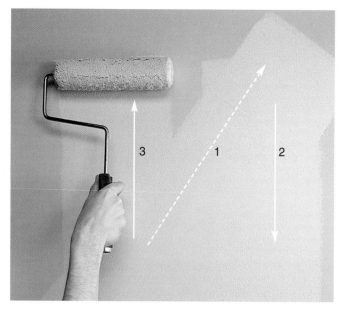

2 Draw the roller straight down (2) from top of the diagonal sweep. Shift the roller to the beginning of the diagonal and roll up (3) to complete the unloading of the roller.

the reservoir to load it with paint. Lift the roller from the paint reservoir, and roll it back-and-forth on the textured ramp to distribute the paint evenly onto the nap. The roller should be full, but not dripping, when lifted from the paint pan.

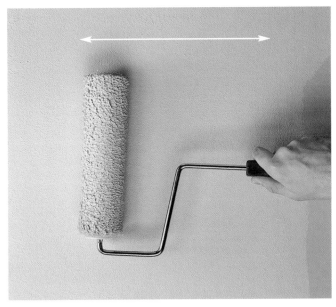

3 Distribute paint over the rest of the section with horizontal back-and-forth strokes.

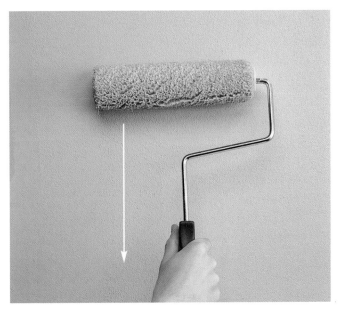

4 Smooth the area by lightly drawing the roller vertically from the top to the bottom of the painted area. Lift the roller and return it to the top of the area after each stroke.

Trim Techniques

When painting an entire room, paint the wood trim first, then paint the walls. Start by painting the inside portions of the trim, and work out toward the walls. On windows, for instance, first paint the edges close to the glass, then paint the surrounding face trim.

Doors should be painted quickly because of the large surface. To avoid lap marks, always paint from dry surfaces back into wet paint. On baseboards, cut in the top edge and work down to the flooring. Plastic floor guards or a wide broadknife can help shield carpet and wood flooring from paint drips.

Alkyds and latex enamels may require two coats. Always sand lightly between coats and wipe with a tack cloth so that the second coat bonds properly.

How to Paint a Window

1 To paint double-hung windows, remove them from their frames, if possible. Newer, spring-mounted windows are re-leased by pushing against the frame (see arrow).

2 Drill holes and insert two 2" nails into the legs of a wooden step ladder. Mount the window easel-style for easy painting. Or, lay the window flat on a bench or sawhorses. Do not paint the sides or bottom of the window sashes.

3 Using a tapered sash brush, begin by painting the wood next to the glass. Use the narrow edge of the brush, and overlap the paint onto the glass to create a weatherseal.

4 Remove excess paint from the glass with a putty knife wrapped in a clean cloth. Rewrap the knife often so that you always wipe with clean fabric. Overlap paint from the sash onto the glass by 1/16."

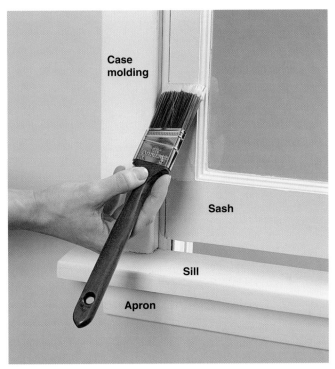

Case molding

Sash

Sill

Apron

5 Paint all flat portions of the sashes, then the case moldings, sill, and apron. Use slow brush strokes, and avoid getting paint between the sash and the frame.

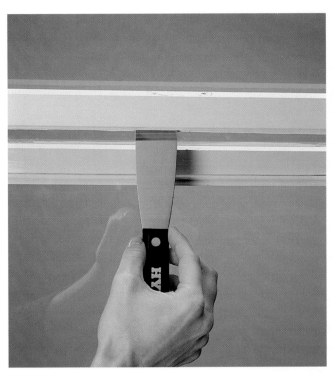

6 If you must paint windows in place, move the painted windows up and down several times during the drying period to keep them from sticking. Use a putty knife to avoid touching the painted surfaces.

How to Paint Doors

1 Remove the door by driving out the lower hinge pin with a screwdriver and hammer. Have a helper hold the door in place. Then, drive out the middle and upper hinge pins.

2 Place the door flat on sawhorses for painting. On paneled doors, paint in the following order, using a brush rather than a roller: 1) recessed panels, 2) horizontal rails, and 3) vertical stiles.

3 Let the painted door dry. If a second coat of paint is needed, sand the first coat lightly and wipe the door with tack cloth before repainting.

4 Seal the unpainted edges of the door with a clear wood sealer to prevent moisture from entering the wood. Water can cause wood to warp and swell.

Tips for Painting Trim

Protect wall and floor surfaces with a wide wallboard knife or a plastic shielding tool.

Wipe all of the paint off of the wallboard knife or shielding tool each time it is moved.

Paint both sides of cabinet doors. This provides an even moisture seal and prevents warping.

Paint deep patterned surfaces with a stiff-bristled brush, like this stenciling brush. Use small circular strokes to penetrate recesses.

Ceiling & Wall Techniques

For a smooth finish on large wall and ceiling areas, paint in small sections. First use a paint-brush to cut in the edge, then immediately roll the section before moving on. If brushed edges are left to dry before the large surfaces are rolled, visible lap marks will be left on the finished wall. Working in natural light makes it easier to spot missed areas.

Choose quality paint and tools, and work with a full brush or roller to avoid lap marks and to ensure full coverage. Keep the roller speed slow to minimize paint splattering.

Tips for Painting Ceilings & Walls

Paint to a wet edge. Cut in the edge on small sections with a paint-brush just before rolling, then move on to the next section. With two painters, let one cut in with a brush while the other rolls the large areas.

Minimize brush marks. Slide the roller cover slightly off of the roller cage when rolling near wall corners or a ceiling line. Brushed areas dry to a different finish than rolled paint.

How to Paint Ceilings

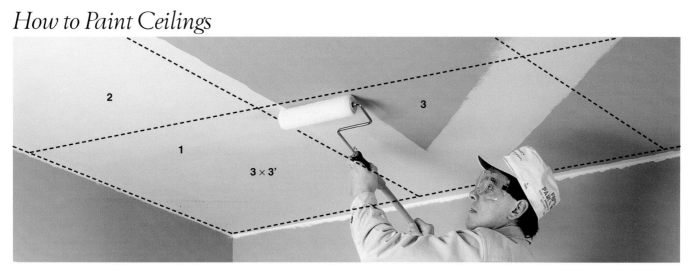

Paint ceilings with a roller handle extension. Use eye protection while painting overhead. Start at the corner farthest from the entry door. Paint the ceiling along the narrow end in 3 × 3' sections, cutting in the edges with a brush before rolling. Apply the paint with a diagonal stroke. Distribute the paint evenly with back-and-forth strokes. For the final smoothing strokes, roll each section toward the wall containing the entry door, lifting the roller at the end of each sweep.

How to Paint Walls

Paint walls in 2 × 4' sections. Start in an upper corner, cutting in the ceiling and wall corners with a brush, then rolling the section. Make the initial diagonal roller stroke from the bottom of the section upward, to avoid dripping paint. Distribute the paint evenly with horizontal strokes, then finish with downward sweeps of the roller. Next, cut in and roll the section directly underneath. Continue with adjacent areas, cutting in and rolling the top sections before the bottom sections. Roll all finish strokes toward the floor.

Painting Techniques 111

Texture Painting

*T*exture paints offer a decorating alternative to either flat paints or wallcoverings. The variety of possible effects you can achieve is limited only by your imagination. Texture paints are available in either premixed latex formulations or in dry powder form. Premixed latex texture paints are fine for producing light stipple patterns, but powder textures are a better choice for creating heavier adobe or stucco finishes. Powder textures are available in 25-lb. bags and must be mixed with water, using a paint mixer bit and power drill.

Practice texturing on cardboard until you get the pattern you want. Remember that the depth of the texture depends on the stiffness of the texture paint, the amount applied to the surface, and the type of tool used to create the texture.

How to Texture Paint

Create a swirl pattern with a whisk broom. Apply the texture paint with a roller, then use the broom to create the design.

Use a long-nap roller to make this stipple texture effect. For different patterns, vary the pressure on the roller and amount of texture paint on the surface.

Trowel texture material onto the surface, and pile the material in ridges to create an adobe pattern.

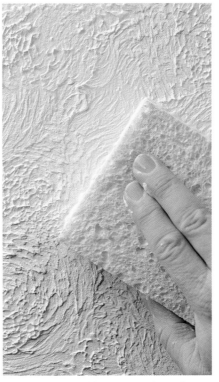

Dab, drag, or swirl a sponge through texture paint to create an endless variety of texture patterns. Or, let the first course dry, then sponge another color on top for a two-tone stucco effect.

Create a crowsfoot design by applying texture paint with a roller, brushing it out level, then randomly striking the surface with the flat side of the brush.

Press the flat side of a trowel into texture paint and pull it away to create a stomp design.

Trowel over a texture pattern when the paint has partially dried, to flatten peaks and achieve a brocade design. Clean the trowel between strokes with a wet brush or sponge.

Cleanup

*A*t the end of a paint job you may choose to throw away the roller covers, but the paint pans, roller handles, and brushes can be cleaned and stored for future use. Stray paint drips can be wiped away if they are still wet. A putty knife or razor will remove many dried paint spots on hardwood or glass. Remove stubborn paint from most surfaces with a chemical cleaner.

Cleaning products include (from left): chemical cleaner, spinner tool, cleaner tool for brushes and roller covers.

Use a spinner tool to remove paint and solvent. Wash the roller cover or brush with solvent, then attach it to the spinner. Pumping the handle throws liquids out of the roller cover or brush. Hold the spinner inside a cardboard box or 5-gallon bucket to catch paint and avoid splatters.

Cleanup Tips

Comb brush bristles with the spiked side of a cleaner tool. This aligns the bristles so they dry properly.

Scrape paint from a roller cover with the curved side of cleaner tool. Remove as much paint as possible before washing the tools with solvent.

Store brushes in their original wrappers, or fold the bristles inside brown wrapping paper. Store washed roller covers on end to avoid flattening the nap.

Remove dried splatters with a chemical cleaner. Before using cleaner, test an inconspicuous area to make sure the surface is colorfast.

Wallcovering Techniques

Wallcovering can be the single most important element in a decorating scheme, setting the style of the room and gracefully pulling together the chosen color scheme. Although many people joke about the difficulty of applying wallcovering, with the right tools, materials, and techniques, two people can paper a room as well as a professional.

This section will walk you through the wallcovering process, from selecting the most appropriate type of wallcovering, to hanging the product on walls and ceilings. There are also easy-to-follow charts that simplify the task of measuring and estimating for wallcovering.

The following pages contain numerous professional tips that will improve your efficiency and help you achieve flawless results. For instance, you will learn how to create a hanging plan and mark the walls before you begin hanging strips. The hanging plan makes easy work of matching patterns, making sure seams line up with corners, and positioning partial strips in inconspicuous areas.

When you are ready to begin wallcovering, the step-by-step instructions will show you how to prepare the strips and hang them on walls or ceilings. You will also find methods for wallcovering around corners, doors, windows, pipes, radiators, fixtures, and even archways. There are also techniques for finishing switchplates and receptacles and hanging wallcovering borders and panels.

Wallcovering Selection

Very few modern "wallpapers" are actually made of paper. Today's wallcoverings may be made of vinyl, vinyl-coated paper or cloth, textiles, natural grasses, foil, or mylar. Vinyl or coated vinyl coverings are the easiest to hang, clean, and remove. Other types of wallcoverings can give a room a unique look but may require special handling. Your choice of wallcovering depends on the needs of the room and on your confidence and ability with wallcovering.

Types of Wallcovering

Vinyl wallcoverings are made with a continuous flexible film, often applied over a fabric or paper backing. Some vinyls successfully duplicate the effect of natural grasscloth or textile wallcoverings. Vinyl wallcoverings with preapplied adhesives are a good choice because they are easy to apply, clean, and remove.

Foils or mylars are coated with a thin, flexible metallic film. These highly reflective wallcoverings add brightness to a room, but they require careful handling. Foils also reveal all wall flaws, so surface preparation must be perfect.

Grasscloths are imported wallcoverings that use natural plant fibers. Because they reflect little light, grasscloths soften the appearance of a room. They are a good choice for flawed, irregular walls. Hang them with clear adhesive. Never use water to rinse grasscloths.

Fabric wallcoverings are made of woven textiles. Fabrics are easy to hang because there is no pattern to match, but they may be difficult to clean.

Embossed wallcoverings are stamped with a relief pattern for an elegant, formal appearance. Never use a seam roller on embossed wallcoverings: they can be easily damaged.

Tips for Choosing Wallcovering

Removability: Strippable wallcoverings (left) can be pulled away from the wall by hand, leaving little or no film or residue. Peelable wallcoverings (right) can be removed but may leave a thin paper layer on the wall, which can usually be removed with soap and water. Check the back of the sample or the wallcovering package for its strippability rating. Choose a strippable product to make future redecorating easier.

Washability: Washable wallcoverings can be cleaned with mild soap and water and a sponge. Scrubbable wallcoverings are durable enough to be scrubbed with a soft brush. Choose scrubbable wallcoverings for heavy-use areas.

Application: Prepasted wallcoverings (left) are factory-coated with water-base adhesive that is activated when wallcovering is wetted in a water tray. Unpasted wallcoverings (right) must be coated with an adhesive for hanging. As well as being easier to prepare, prepasted products are just as durable as those requiring an adhesive coat.

Dye-lot: Jot down dye-lot numbers for reference. If you need additional rolls, order from the same dye-lot to avoid slight color differences.

Packaging: Wallcoverings are sold in continuous triple, double, and single-roll bolts.

Patterns: There is always more waste with large patterns. A wallcovering with a large drop pattern can be more expensive to hang than one with a smaller repeat. With large designs, it may also be difficult to avoid pattern interruptions at baseboards or corners.

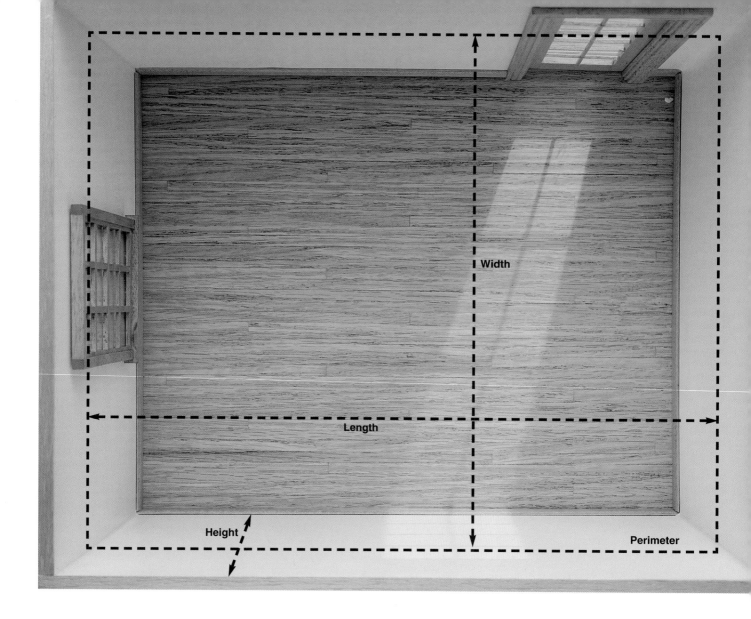

Width

Length

Height

Perimeter

Measuring & Estimating Methods

With a few room measurements and the information listed on the wallcovering package, you can estimate the correct amount of wallcovering to buy. The procedure given on these two pages will help you calculate the square footage of your walls and ceilings and show you how to find the per-roll coverage of wallcovering.

Because of normal trimming waste, the actual per-roll coverage of wallcovering will be at least 15% less than the coverage listed on the package. The waste percentage can be higher depending on how much space it takes for the wallcovering pattern to repeat itself. This "pattern repeat" measurement is listed on

the wallcovering package. You can compensate for this extra waste factor by adding the pattern repeat measurement to the wall height measurement of the room.

Measure the room:

Walls: Measure the *length* of the wall, to the nearest ½ ft. (Add the length of all the walls to find the perimeter, if the entire room will be wallcovered.) Include window and door openings in wall measurements. Measure the *height* of surfaces to be covered, to the nearest ½ ft. Do not include baseboards or crown moldings in height measurement. **Ceilings:** Measure the length and the *width* of ceiling to the nearest ½ ft.

How to Measure Unusual Surfaces

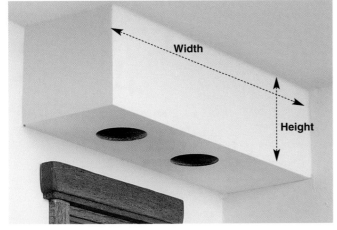

Soffits: If you are covering the sides of a soffit, add the width and height of each side into the wall measurement.

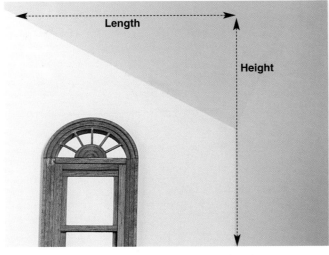

Triangular walls: Measure as though the surface is square: length × height.

Wallcovering packages or pattern books give per-roll coverage, in square feet, and the drop pattern repeat measurement.

How to Figure Actual Per-roll Coverage

1) Total per-roll coverage (square feet)	
2) Adjust for waste factor	×.85
3) **Actual per-roll coverage** (square feet)	=

How to Calculate Rolls Needed for a Ceiling

1) Room length (feet)	
2) Wallcovering pattern repeat (feet)	+
3) Adjusted length (feet)	=
4) Room width (feet)	×
5) Ceiling area (square feet)	=
6) Actual per-roll coverage (figured above; square feet)	÷
7) **Number of rolls needed for ceiling**	=

How to Calculate Rolls Needed for Walls

1) Wall height (feet)	
2) Wallcovering pattern repeat (feet)	+
3) Adjusted height (feet)	=
4) Wall length; or room perimeter (feet)	×
5) Wall area (square feet)	=
6) Actual per-roll coverage (figured above; square feet)	÷
7) Number of rolls	=
8) Add 1 roll for each archway or recessed window	+
9) **Number of rolls needed for walls**	=

Paint pail

Natural sponge

Water tray

Bubblestick

Paint tray & roller

Smoothing brushes

Smoothing tool

Wallboard knife

Seam roller

Razor knife

Wallcovering scissors

Tools

Many of the tools for hanging wallcovering are common items you may already own. Keep a supply of #2 pencils and a pencil sharpener handy for precise marking when laying out and cutting wallcovering. Never use an ink marker or ballpoint pen, because the ink might bleed through the wet wallcovering.

Use a bubblestick or carpenter's level for establishing plumb lines and as a straightedge for cutting. Don't use a chalk line: the chalk can smear the new wallcovering or ooze through the seams. Trim wallcoverings with a razor knife that features breakaway tips. Buy noncorrosive paint pails for holding wash water, and use a natural or high-quality plastic sponge to avoid damaging the wallcovering.

Wallcovering adhesives can be applied with an ordinary paint roller, but you will need a smoothing tool to flatten the wallcovering strips as you hang them, and a seam roller to fix the joints between strips. Ask your dealer about the proper tools for your wallcovering.

Smoothing brushes come in various nap lengths. Use a short nap brush for smoothing out vinyl wallcoverings. A soft, long nap brush is used for fragile wallcoverings, like grasscloths.

A razor knife with breakaway blades is used for trimming wallcovering at ceilings, baseboards, corners, windows, and doors. Renew tips often to avoid snagging and tearing the wallcovering.

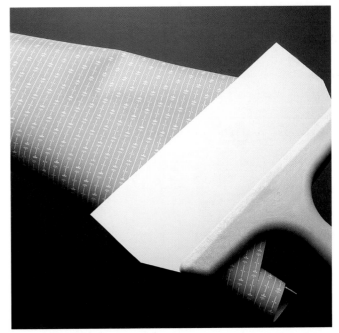

Use a wide broadknife to hold wallcoverings tightly while trimming overlaps in corners and against window or door casings. A narrower broadknife may work better for intricate corners.

(continued next page)

Wallcovering Tools *(continued)*

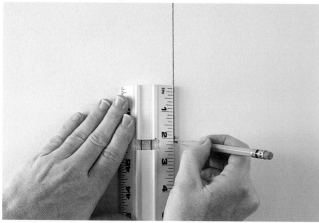

A bubblestick or carpenter's level is used to mark verticals for a plumb line, and doubles as a straightedge for cutting. Use a level instead of a chalk line: chalk can bleed through wallcovering seams.

Use wallcovering scissors to trim wallcovering at the seam where wall and ceiling coverings meet. A razor knife may puncture the underlying ceiling strip.

A wallcoverer's table provides a flat working surface. Wallcovering stores lend or rent tables. Or, you can make your own by placing a sheet of plywood on sawhorses.

Hold a straightedge tightly against the booked wallcovering strip and cut with a sharp razor knife to form partial strips for corners. Hold the knife blade straight while cutting the strip.

A wallcovering tray holds water for wetting prepasted wallcovering strips.

A sponge and bucket are used for rinsing down strips. Use a natural or quality synthetic sponge.

Use a paint roller or paste brush to apply adhesive to the backs of unpasted wallcovering strips.

Materials

Before hanging wallcovering, the wall surfaces must be both sealed and sized to prevent the adhesives from soaking into the wall surface. Today's premixed primer-sealers do both jobs with a single application.

If your wallcovering is not pre-pasted, you will need one or more types of adhesive. For most vinyl or vinyl-backed wallcoverings, choose a heavy-duty premixed vinyl adhesive that contains a mildew inhibitor. Vinyl wallcoverings also require a special vinyl-on-vinyl adhesive for areas where the wallcovering strips overlap, such as around wall corners and archways.

When hanging specialty wallcoverings, you may need special adhesives. Natural grasscloths, for instance, require a clear-drying adhesive that will not soak through and stain the fibers. Check the wallcovering label or ask your dealer about the correct adhesive for your application.

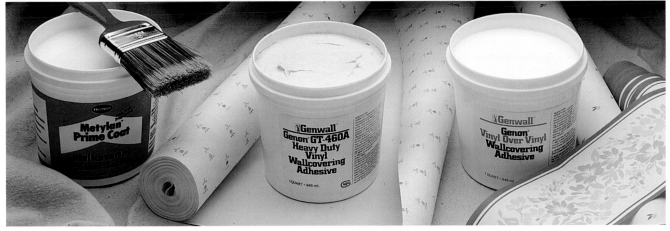

Latex primer-sealers seal and size walls in one application. These are available as a powder or in premixed form. Heavy-duty vinyl adhesive is used to hang vinyl or vinyl-backed wall-coverings. Vinyl-on-vinyl adhesive fastens lap seams on vinyl wallcoverings. It is also used to apply vinyl borders over vinyl wallcoverings.

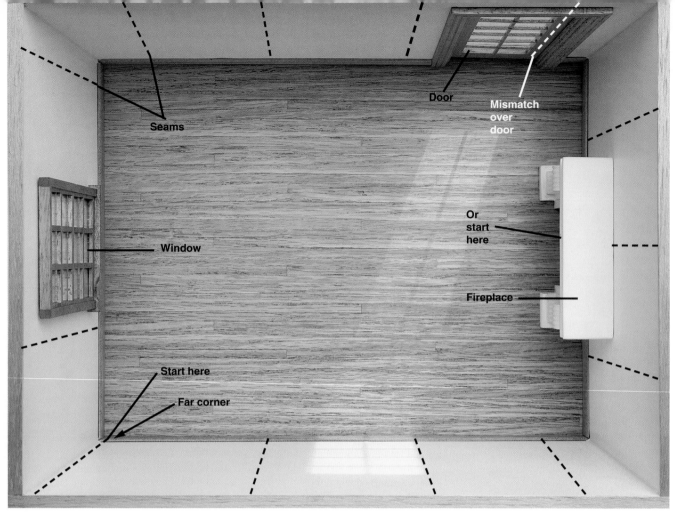

Sketch out the locations of the seams. Any mismatch should be in an inconspicuous area, like behind a door.

The Hanging Plan

Tips for Planning Seams

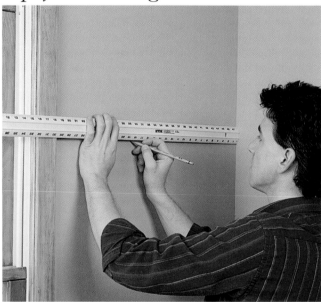

Plan the mismatch. If the room has no obvious focal point, start at the corner farthest from the entry. Measure out a distance equal to the wallcovering width and mark a point. Work in both directions, marking out points where the seams will fall.

When hanging any patterned wallcovering, there will be one seam where a full strip meets a partial strip. The pattern will usually mismatch at this point. Plan this mismatched seam in an inconspicuous spot, like behind a door or above an entrance.

Sketch out seam lines before you begin. Avoid placing seams that will be difficult to handle. A seam that falls close to the edge of a window or fireplace complicates the job. At corners, wallcovering should always overlap slightly onto the opposite wall. If one or more seams falls in a bad spot, adjust your plumb line a few inches to compensate.

Start at a focal point, like a fireplace or large window. Center a plumb line on the focal point, then sketch a wall covering plan in both directions from the center line.

Adjust your plan for corners that fall exactly on seam lines. Make sure you have at least ½" overlap on inside corners, and 1" on outside corners.

Adjust for seams that fall in difficult locations, like near the edges of windows or doors. Shift your starting point so that the seams leave you with workable widths of wallcovering around these obstacles.

Plan a ceiling layout so that any pattern interruption will be along the least conspicuous side of the room. Pattern interruptions occur on the last ceiling strip, so begin hanging covering opposite the side where the room is entered.

Reroll each wallcovering roll with the pattern side in. Inspect the pattern surface for color and design flaws. Return any flawed rolls to your dealer.

Wallcovering Handling Techniques

For durability and easy application, choose a quality prepasted vinyl wallcovering whenever possible. Clear the room of all furniture that can be easily removed, and layer newspapers or drop cloths next to the walls. For easy handling, rent a wall-coverer's table, or make your own (page 124).

Shut off the electricity to the room at the main service panel, and check all switches and outlet receptacles to be sure the power is off. Remove the receptacle and switch coverplates. Cover the receptacle slots with masking tape to keep out water and adhesive.

For the best visibility and drying conditions, work during the daylight hours. And have another person help you whenever possible. A helper is especially useful when covering ceilings.

As you hang the wallcovering, make sure each strip is perfectly positioned before going on to the next. You can adjust the strips once they are on the wall, but make the initial placement carefully, as too much adjusting can stretch some coverings and may wrinkle and tear.

Tip:

Some premium wallcoverings have unprinted side edges (called "selvages") that protect the roll. The selvages must be cut off the wallcovering strip with a razor knife and straightedge before hanging. The selvages may have printed guide marks for precise cutting.

How to Measure & Cut Wallcovering Strips

1 Hold the wallcovering strip against the wall. Make sure there is a full pattern at the ceiling line and that the strip overlaps the ceiling and baseboard by about 2". Cut the strip to length with scissors.

2 For the next strips, find the pattern match with the previously hung strip. Then, measure and cut the new strip with about 2" of excess at each end.

How to Handle Prepasted Wallcovering

How to Handle Unpasted Wallcovering

1 Fill a water tray half full of lukewarm water. Roll the cut strip loosely with the pattern side in. Soak the roll in the tray as directed by the manufacturer, usually about 1 minute.

2 Holding one edge of the strip with both hands, lift the wallcovering from the water. Watch the pasted side to make sure the strip is evenly wetted. Book the strip as indicated (page 130).

Lay the strip with the pattern side down on a wallcoverer's table or flat surface. Apply adhesive evenly to the strip, using a paint roller. Wipe any adhesive from the table before preparing the next strip.

How to Book Wallcovering Strips

"Book" wallcovering by folding both ends of the strip into the center, with the pasted side in. Do not crease the folds. Let the strip stand (cure) for about 10 minutes. Some wallcoverings should not be booked: follow the manufacturer's directions.

For ceiling strips or wallcovering borders, use an "accordion" book. Fold the strip back and forth with the pasted side in for easy handling. Let the strip stand (cure) for about 10 minutes.

How to Position & Smooth Wallcovering

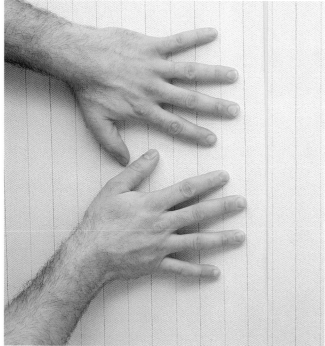

1 Unfold the booked strip and position it lightly with its edge butted against a plumb line or previous strip. Use flat palms to slide the strip precisely into place. Flatten the top of the strip with a smoothing brush.

2 Beginning at the top, smooth the wallcovering out from the center in both directions. Check for bubbles, and make sure the seams are properly butted. Pull the strip away and reposition it, if necessary.

How to Trim Wallcovering

1 Hold the wallcovering against molding or the ceiling with a wide wallboard knife. Cut away excess with a sharp razor knife. Keep the knife blade in place while changing the position of the wallboard knife.

2 With wallcovered ceilings, crease the wall strips with a broad knife, then cut along the crease with scissors. Cutting with a razor knife may puncture the ceiling strip.

How to Roll Seams

Let the strips stand for about ½ hour. Then, roll the seam gently with a seam roller. Do not press out the adhesive by rolling to much or too forcefully. Do not roll seams on foils, fabrics, or embossed wallcoverings. Instead, tap the seams gently with a smoothing brush.

How to Rinse Wallcovering

Use clear water and a sponge to rinse adhesive from the surface. Change the water after every 3 or 4 strips. Do not let water run along the seams. Do not use water on grasscloths, embossed wallcoverings, or fabrics.

How to Wallcover a Ceiling

1 Measure the width of the wallcovering strip and subtract ½". Near a corner, measure this distance away from the wall at several points, and mark points on the ceiling with a pencil.

Ceiling & Wall Techniques

Wallcovering a ceiling is easier if you have another person to help you. Let your helper hold one end of the accordion-folded strips as you place the other end.

Dust your hands with talcum powder when handling dry wallcovering, to avoid smudges. When planning a ceiling job, remember that the pattern on the last wallcovering strip may be broken by the ceiling line. Since the least visible ceiling edge is usually on the entry wall, begin hanging ceiling strips at the far end of the room, and work back toward the entryway.

If you plan to cover the walls as well as the ceiling, remember that the ceiling pattern can blend perfectly into only one wall. Plan the ceiling job so the strips will blend into your chosen "match" wall.

2 Using the marks as guides, draw a guide line along the length of the ceiling with a pencil and straightedge. Cut and prepare the first wallcovering strip (page 128).

3 Working in small sections, position the strip against the guide line. Overlap the side wall by ½", and the end wall by 2". Flatten the strip with the smoothing brush as you work. Trim each strip after it is smoothed.

4 Cut out a small wedge of wallcovering in the corner so that the strip will lie flat. Press the wallcovering into the corner with a wallboard knife.

5 If the end walls will also be covered, trim the ceiling overlap to ½". Leave a ½" overlap on all walls that will be covered with matching wallcovering.

On walls that will not be covered, trim the excess by holding a wallboard knife against the corner and cutting with a sharp razor knife. Continue hanging strips, butting the edges so that the pattern matches.

How to Wallcover Walls

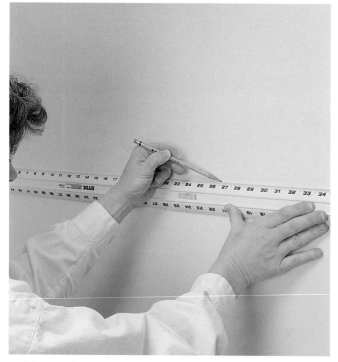

1 Measure from a corner the distance equal to the wallcovering width minus ½", and mark a point. Sketch out the seam locations, and make adjustments, if necessary (see The Hanging Plan, pages 126–127).

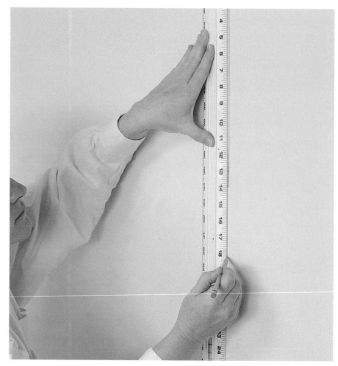

2 Draw a plumb line at the marked point, using a bubblestick. For a wall that must match the pattern of a wallcovered ceiling, draw the plumb line straight down from first ceiling seam.

3 Cut and prepare the first strip (page 128). First, unfold the top portion of the booked strip. Position the strip against the plumb line so that the strip overlaps onto the ceiling by about 2". Make sure there is a full pattern at the ceiling line.

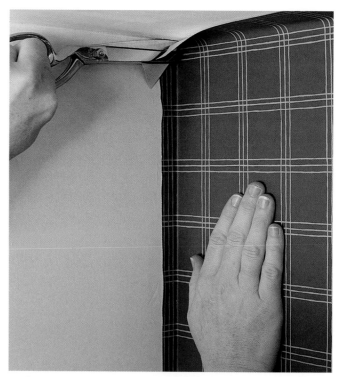

4 Snip the top corner of the strip so that the wallcovering wraps around the corner without wrinkling. Use open palms to slide the strip into position, with the edge butted against the plumb line. Press the strip flat with a smoothing brush.

5 Unfold the bottom of the strip, and use flat palms to position the strip against the plumb line. Press the strip flat with a smoothing brush. Check carefully for bubbles.

6 Trim excess wallcovering with a sharp razor knife. If the ceiling is wallcovered, crease the edge of the wall strip with a wallboard knife, then trim along the crease with scissors to avoid punctures. Rinse any adhesive from the surfaces.

7 Hang additional strips, butting the edges so that the pattern matches. Let the strips stand for about ½ hour, then use a seam roller to lightly roll the seam. On embossed wallcoverings or fabrics, tap the seams gently with smoothing brush.

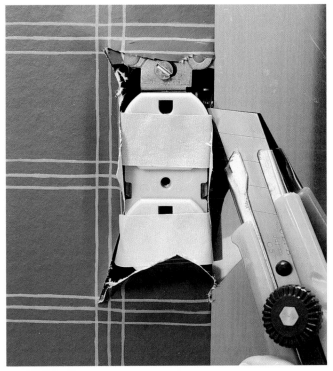

8 With the power turned off, hang the wallcovering over any outlets and switches. Make small diagonal cuts to expose the outlet. Trim the wallcovering back to the edges of the electrical box with a razor knife.

How to Wallcover Around an Inside Corner

1 Cut and prepare a full strip (page 128). While the strip cures, measure from the edge of the previous strip to the corner at the top, middle, and bottom of the wall. Add ½" to the longest of these measurements.

2 Align the edges of the booked strip. From the edge, measure, at two points, a distance equal to the measurement found in Step 1. Hold a straightedge against the two marked points, and cut the wallcovering strip, using a sharp razor knife.

3 Position the strip on the wall with the pattern matching the previous strip. Overlap the ceiling by about 2". Using open palms, carefully butt the edges of the strips. The strip will overlap slightly onto uncovered wall.

4 Make small corner slits at the top and bottom of the strip to wrap the overlap around the corner without wrinkling. Flatten the strip with a smoothing brush, then trim the excess at the ceiling and baseboard.

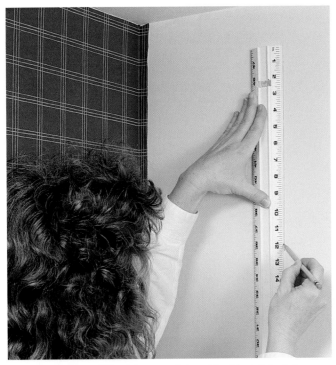

5 Measure the width of the remaining strip. Mark this distance from the corner onto the uncovered wall. Draw a plumb line from the ceiling to the floor on the new wall, using a bubblestick.

6 Position the strip on the wall with the cut edge in the corner and the factory edge against the new plumb line. Press the strip flat with a smoothing brush. Trim the excess at the ceiling and baseboard.

7 If you are using vinyl wallcovering, peel back the edge and apply vinyl-on-vinyl adhesive to the lap seam. Press the seam area flat. Let the strips stand for ½ hour, then roll the seams, and rinse the area, using a damp sponge.

Variation: Outside corners can usually be wrapped around without cutting the strip and drawing a new plumb line. If corner is not plumb, follow the directions for inside corners, except add 1" to the Step 1 measurement to allow for a wider wrap.

Window & Door Techniques

Do not try to precut wall covering strips to fit the shape of windows or doors. Hang a full strip right over the casing, then smooth the strip before trimming the edges along the door or window. Make diagonal cuts to fit the wallcovering around sharp corners. To avoid damaging the wood on these diagonal cuts, use scissors instead of a razor knife.

If short strips are hung directly above and below an opening, make sure they are hung exactly vertical to ensure a good pattern fit with the next full strip. Do not trim the short strips until the last full strip has been hung. This allows for small adjustments in case of slight mismatches.

How to Wallcover Around Windows & Doors

1 Position the strip on the wall, running over the window casing. Butt the seam against the edge of the previous strip.

2 Smooth the flat areas of wallcovering with a smoothing brush. Press the strip tightly against casing.

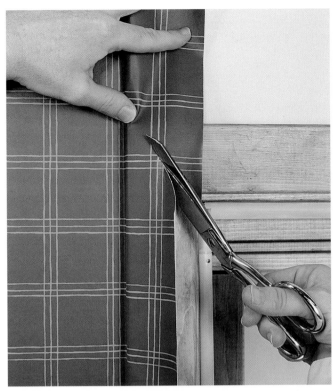

3 Use scissors to cut diagonally from the edge of the strip to the corner of the casing. Make a similar cut in the bottom corner, if you are wallcovering around a window.

4 Use scissors to trim away excess wallcovering to about 1" around the inside of the frame. Smooth the wallcovering and press out any bubbles as you work.

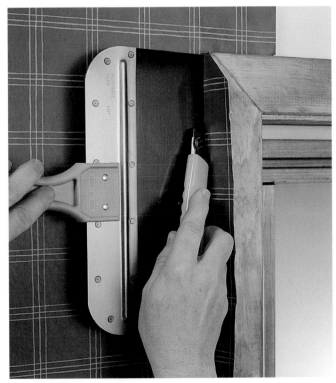

5 Hold the wallcovering against the casing with a wallboard knife, and trim excess with a sharp razor knife. Trim overlaps at the ceiling and baseboard. Rinse the wallcovering and casings, using a damp sponge.

6 Cut short strips for sections above and below the window. You may find scraps that will match the pattern and fit these spaces. Hang small strips exactly vertical to ensure a pattern match with the next full strip.

(continued next page)

Wallcovering Techniques   139

7 Cut and prepare the next full strip. Position it on the wall with its edge butting the previous strip so that the pattern matches.

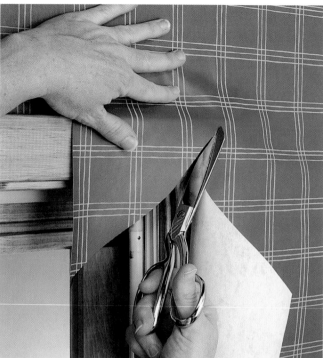

8 Snip the top and bottom corners diagonally from the edge of the strip to the corners of the casing. Trim away excess wallcovering to about 1" around the inside of the window or door frame.

9 Match the seam on the bottom half of the strip. Trim the excess wallcovering to about 1" with scissors. Flatten the strip with a smoothing brush.

10 Hold the wallcovering against the casing with a wall board knife, and cut the excess with a sharp razor knife. Trim the overlaps at the ceiling and baseboard. Rinse the wallcovering and casings, using a damp sponge.

How to Wallcover a Recessed Window

1 Hang the wallcovering strips so they overlap the recess. Smooth the strips and trim the excess at the baseboard and ceiling. To wrap the top and bottom of the recess, make a horizontal cut at the halfway point to within ½" of the wall.

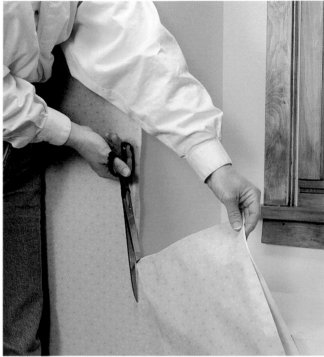

2 From the horizontal cut (Step 1), make vertical cuts to the top and bottom of the recess. Make small diagonal cuts to the corners of the recess.

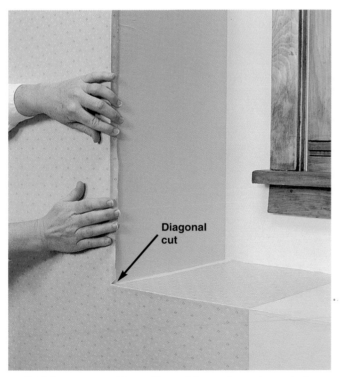

Diagonal cut

3 Fold the upper and lower flaps of the wallcovering onto the recessed surfaces. Smooth the strips and trim them at the back edge. Wrap the vertical edge around the corner. Hang wallcovering around the window, if needed (pages 138–139).

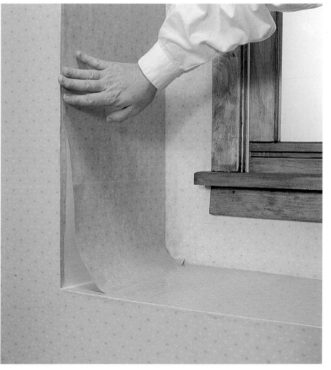

4 Measure, cut, and prepare a matching piece of wallcovering to cover the side of the recess. The side piece should slightly overlap the top and bottom of the recess and the wrapped vertical edge. Use vinyl-on-vinyl adhesive to glue the overlapped seams.

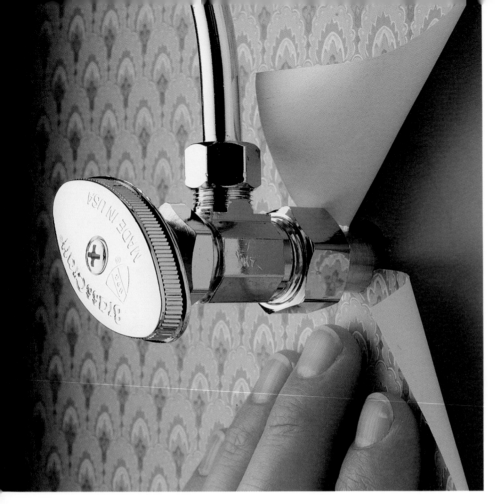

Pipe, Radiator, & Fixture Techniques

*H*anging wallcovering around sinks, pipes, and other obstacles requires cutting into wallcovering strips. Hold the strip so that patterns match, and cut from the edge closest to the fixture. If possible, cut along a pattern line to hide the slit. At the end of the slit, cut an opening to fit around the fixture. With wall-mounted sinks, tuck small wallcovering overlaps behind the sink.

How to Wallcover Around a Pipe

1 Pull out the escutcheon from the wall. Hold the wallcovering strip against the wall so that the pattern matches the previous strip. From the closest edge of the strip, cut the slit to reach the pipe.

2 Press the strip flat up to the pipe with a smoothing brush.

3 Cut a hole at the end of the slit to fit around the pipe. Butt the edges of the slit together and brush them smooth.

How to Wallcover Around a Wall-mounted Sink

1 Brush the wallcovering strip up to the edge of the sink. Cut horizontal slits in the wallcovering, leaving a ¼" overlap at the top and bottom of the sink.

2 Trim the wallcovering around the side of the sink, leaving a slight overlap.

3 Smooth the wallcovering. Tuck the excess wallcovering into the crack between the sink and the wall, if possible, or trim the overlap.

How to Wallcover Behind a Radiator

1 Unfold the entire strip and position it on the wall. Smooth the strip from the ceiling to the top of the radiator. Use a flat wooden yardstick to smooth the strip down behind the radiator. Crease the wallcovering along the baseboard with the yardstick.

2 Pull the bottom of the strip up from behind the radiator. Trim the excess wallcovering along the crease line. Smooth the covering back down behind radiator with the yardstick.

How To Wallcover an Archway

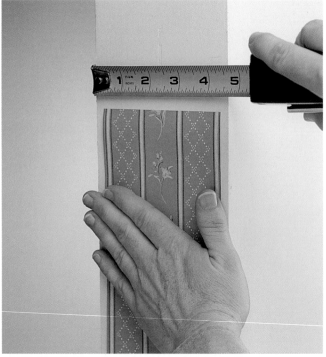

1 Some wallcoverings are available with matching borders that can be used to cover the inside of an archway. Or, measure the inside of the archway and cut the strip from standard wallcovering. The strip should be ¼" narrower than inside surface of archway.

2 Hang the wallcovering on both sides of the archway, with the strips overlapping the archway opening. Smooth the strips and trim the excess at the ceiling and baseboards.

Archway Techniques

Cover the inside surface of an archway with wallcovering after the walls are finished. Wrap the wall strips around the edges of the archway, then hang a matching strip or wallcovering border around the inside surface to cover the wrapped edges. Make a series of small slits in the wall strips along the archway curve so that the wallcovering lies smoothly. Use vinyl-on-vinyl adhesive to hang the archway strip.

3 Use scissors to trim the overlapping wallcovering, leaving about 1" of excess.

4 Make small slits in the wallcovering along the curved portion of the archway, cutting as close as possible to the wall edge.

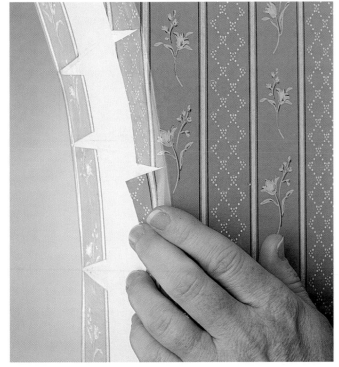

5 Wrap the cut edges inside the archway and press them flat. If the adjacent room will be wallcovered, wrap the wallcovering around the edge of the archway from both sides.

6 Coat the back of the archway strip with vinyl-on-vinyl adhesive. Position the strip along the inside of the archway with a ⅛" space on each edge of the strip. Smooth the strip with a smoothing brush. Rinse the strip, using damp sponge.

Wallcovering Techniques 145

Switch & Outlet Coverplates

*A*s a finishing touch, cover the switch and outlet coverplates with matching wallcovering. For plastic coverplates, use a vinyl-on-vinyl adhesive.

To fully blend the switches and outlets with the wallcovering, paint the receptacle face, switch levers and coverplate screw heads with a coordinating paint. Be sure to turn off the electricity at the main service panel (or breaker box) and test the switches and outlets for power before working on them.

Tip:

If you wallcover the coverplates in guest bathrooms and bedrooms, you may want to install switches with illuminated levers for the benefit of guests.

An easy way to match outlets and switches is to purchase new clear plastic coverplates. Cut the wallcovering to fit into the coverplates, and cut openings for the switch levers and receptacle faces.

How to Cover Switch or Outlet Coverplates

1 Remove the coverplate and reinsert the screws. Cut a patch from scrap wallcovering that matches the area around the switch or outlet. Fasten the patch over the outlet with drafting tape, so that the pattern matches the wall.

2 Rub the surface of patch to emboss the outline of the outlet or switch screws. Remove the patch and mark the embossed reference points in pencil on the back side.

3 Lay the coverplate facedown over the wallcovering patch so that the hole marks line up with the holes in the coverplate. Mark the corners of the coverplate on the patch.

4 Trim the patch ½" wider than the coverplate on all sides. Trim the corners of the patch, cutting just outside of the corner marks.

5 Apply vinyl-on-vinyl adhesive to the coverplate and patch. Attach the coverplate to the wallcovering. Smooth out any bubbles. Wrap the overlap around the back, and tape the edges in place.

6 Use a razor knife to cut the openings in the coverplate. Tape the wallcovering pattern specifications on the back of the coverplate for future reference.

Borders

W allcovering borders are available in a variety of designs, and you can use them to complement any painted or wallcovered wall. Hang a border as a crown molding around a ceiling, or as a frame around windows, doors, or fireplaces. When using a border to outline or frame features of a room, select a border with a nondirectional print, as directional prints may be less appealing when hung upside down.

Many wallcoverings have borders which are colored or patterned to complement the wallcovering design. Or you can create your own border by cutting narrow strips from full-size wallcovering. Some border designs have matching or coordinating corner pieces to add a finishing touch. To make custom corner pieces or end accents, cut design motifs from extra sheets of wallcovering or border strips, and glue them to the border using vinyl-on-vinyl adhesive.

To determine the placement of a border, cut a strip of border several feet long. Tape the strip to the wall in different locations to help you visualize how the placement will affect the proportions of the room. A border placed at the top of a wall, for example, draws the eye upward to the ceiling. Positioned at picture level, a border can make a high ceiling seem lower. To use a border as a chair rail, position the center of the border one-third of the distance up from the floor.

When hanging borders, start in an inconspicuous area, such as at the hinge-side of an entry door.This is important because a mismatch usually occurs where the last border segment meets the first. You can run a border in a continuous band around doors and windows using a simple overlapping technique to cut perfect miter joints at the corners.

Wallcovering borders are sold by the yard or prepackaged in 5-yd. to 7-yd. spools. To estimate the yardage you will need, measure the areas where the border will run. Allow extra yardage for matching a pattern and for normal trimming waste. For each mitered corner, add at least twice the border width, plus 2".

How to Hang Wallcovering Borders

1 If you are positioning the border on the wall other than along the ceiling or baseboard, draw a light pencil line around the room at the desired height, using a carpenter's level. Cut the first border strip. Prepare the strip, using border adhesive and following the methods for preparing unpasted wallcovering (page 129).

2 Begin at the least conspicuous corner, overlapping the border onto the adjacent wall by ½". Have a helper hold the accordion-booked border while you apply it and smooth it with a smoothing brush.

3 At the inside corner, create a ¼" tuck from the overhang. Apply the adjoining border strip, trimming it with a razor knife.

4 Peel back the tucked strip, and smooth the strip around the corner, overlapping the border on the adjacent wall. Press the border flat. Apply seam adhesive to the lapped seam, if necessary.

5 Where seams fall in the middle of a wall, overlap the border strips so the patterns match. Cut through both layers, using a razor knife and a wallboard knife. Peel back the borders and remove the cut ends. Press the strips flat. Roll the seam after ½ hour, and rinse with a sponge.

6 Trim the border at door or window casings by holding the border against the outer edge of the casing with a wallboard knife and trimming the excess with a sharp razor knife. Rinse the border and casing, using a damp sponge.

How to Miter Border Corners

1 Apply the horizontal border strips, extending them past the corners a distance greater than the width of the border. Apply the vertical border strips, overlapping the horizontal strips.

2 Hold a straightedge along the points where the border strips intersect, and cut through both layers, using a razor knife. Peel back the strips and remove the cut ends.

3 Press the border back in place. Lightly roll the seam after ½ hour. Rinse any adhesive from the border, using a damp sponge.

Wallcovering Techniques 151

Panels

By combining wallcovering and coordinating borders, you can create decorative wall panels to add interest and elegance to painted walls. Use the panels to divide large walls into smaller sections, or position them to highlight pictures or mirrors. Make the panels identical in size, or alternate wide panels with narrow ones.

For a balanced appearance, space the panels evenly on the wall, leaving slightly more space below the panel than above. Begin by planning the placement of the most dominant or conspicuous panels first. It may help to sketch the room on graph paper, taking into account the position of windows, doors, and furnishings. Also account for any pattern repeat in the wallcovering to allow for matching patterns.

Before you cut any wallcovering, make false panels from butcher paper and tape them to the walls according to your plan. Once the false panels are in place, use them to draw layout lines for the real panels.

How to Make Wallcovering Panels

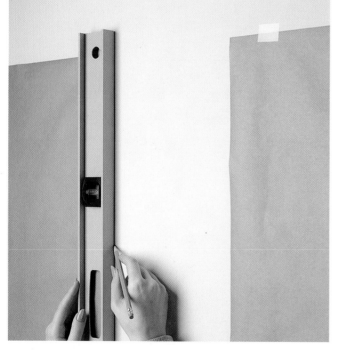

1 Determine the size and position of the wallcovering panels by cutting and taping paper to the wall. Using a pencil and a carpenter's level, mark the outline of the panels on the wall. Measure and record the dimensions of each panel.

2 Cut a strip of wallcovering for the center of each panel to size, using a framing square to ensure 90° angles at the corners. Prepare the strip following the instructions on page 129.

3 Unfold the top portion of the booked strip. Press it lightly on the wall, aligning the edges with the marked lines. Use flat palms to slide the strip into place. Press the top of the strip flat with a smoothing brush, and check for bubbles.

4 Unfold the bottom half of the strip. Use flat palms to position the strip against the marked lines. Press the strip flat with smoothing brush, checking for bubbles.

5 Cut and apply any remaining strips, matching the pattern and butting the seams. Roll the seam after 1/2 hour. Rinse any adhesive from the wallcovering and wall, using clear water and a damp sponge. Prepare the border, using border adhesive and following the methods for preparing unpasted wallcovering (page 129).

6 Apply the border strips in a clockwise direction, starting at the least conspicuous corner. Butt the inner edges of the border to the panel edges. Miter the corners (page 151). Smooth the first corner only lightly until the final strip is applied. Roll the outer edges of the border and seams after 1/2 hour.

Wallcovering Techniques   153

Finishing Touches

How to Fix a Bubble

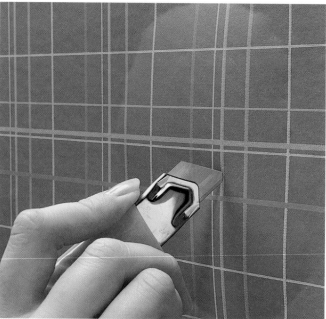

After you have finished wallcovering a room, check for areas to touch up while the job is still fresh. Pay special attention to the seams: if you rolled the seams too hard, or rolled them before the adhesive set, you may have squeezed too much adhesive from under the edges of the covering. These edges will look tight while they are wet but will bubble after the covering is dry. Reglue the edges of the seam as shown.

Inspect the wallcovering for bubbles, loose spots, and other flaws, using a strong sidelight. Stand close to the wall and look down its length, against the light.

1 Cut a slit through the bubble, using a sharp razor knife. If there is a pattern in the wallcovering, cut along a line in the pattern to hide the slit.

2 Insert the tip of a glue applicator through the slit and apply adhesive sparingly to the wall under the wallcovering.

3 Press the wallcovering gently to rebond it. Use a clean, damp sponge to press the flap down and wipe away excess glue.

How to Patch Wallcovering

1 Fasten a scrap of matching wallcovering over the damaged portion with drafting tape, so that the patterns match.

2 Holding a razor knife blade at a 90° angle to the wall, cut through both layers of wallcovering. If the wallcovering has strong pattern lines, cut along the lines to hide the seams. With less definite patterns, cut irregular lines.

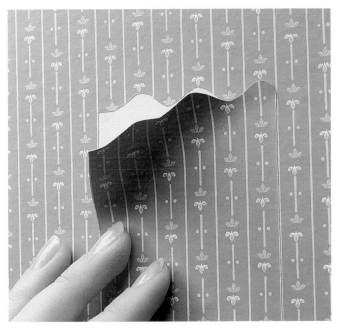

How to Fix a Seam

3 Remove the scrap and patch, then peel away the damaged wallcovering. Apply adhesive to the back of the patch and position it in the hole so that the pattern matches. Rinse the patch area with a damp sponge.

Lift the edge of the wallcovering and insert the tip of a glue applicator under it. Squirt adhesive onto the wall and gently press the seam flat. Let the repair stand for ½ hour, then smooth the seam lightly with a seam roller. Wipe the seam lightly with a damp sponge.

Advanced Painting & Decorating

Painting Advanced Designs & Finishes

*B*eyond the standard process of painting walls and ceilings with a solid color lies a host of advanced painting techniques you can use to add creativity and self-expression to your decorating. In this section, you will learn how to use modern tools and paints with the time-honored techniques mastered by artists and decorators. With the right tools and a little practice, you can master any of these effects, then use your imagination to expand or adapt the techniques for your own custom finish.

First, you will learn about the specialty tools used to create specific effects. You'll learn how to make paint glazes, following given formulas to improve the texture and increase the workability of your paint. From there, it's a simple matter of selecting the design or finish that will add new life to a room or a touch of illusion to a dull surface.

There are over 20 painting techniques in this section, ranging from simple stripe designs to stenciled patterns to a faux moiré finish that captures the beauty and delicate texture of watermarked silk. There are also several finishes for floors. Look through all of the techniques before deciding on one– you may want to combine finishes into one design. For example, you can add depth to the ordered layout of a striped design by painting alternating rows with a textured finish.

For best results with any advanced finish, prepare the surface you will be painting (pages 60–89), and apply a base coat of paint or a primer, if necessary. You can practice the techniques and test your chosen colors by applying the finish to a large piece of mat board. Then, hang the board on the wall for the 24-Hour Test (page 57).

Advanced Painting Tools

Many tools and paintbrushes have been developed for creating specialized decorative painting effects. Depending on how they are used, some tools may create more than one effect. Working with the various tools and learning their capabilities is an important step in becoming a successful faux finisher. Most tools and paintbrushes are available in a range of sizes. As a general rule, use the largest size tool or brush suitable for the surface area.

Some tools and brushes are designed for manipulating the wet glaze on the surface. These include: floggers (A), blending brushes or softeners (B), stipplers (C), and a mottler (D).

Certain faux effects are achieved using removal tools, such as a wood graining rocker (E), overgrainers (F), wipe-out tools (G), and combs (H). Artist's erasers (I) can be notched and used as combs (page 219).

Specialty brushes designed for applying paints and glazes include artist's brushes, such as rounds (J), liners (K), or a dagger (L). These may be used for veining in marble finishes or graining in wood finishes. Stenciling brushes (M) are available in ¼" to 1¼" diameters. Other tools, such as a sea sponge (N) or feathers (O) are also used for applying paints and glazes. A check roller (P) is a specialty tool used for applying pore structure in a faux oak finish.

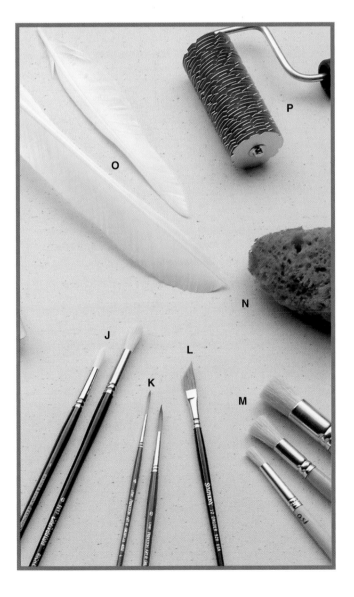

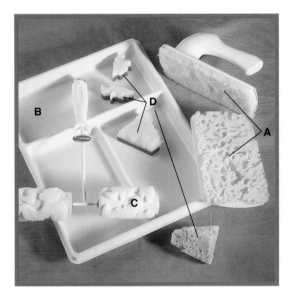

Easy-to-use decorative painting tools (above) are available in kits, which you can add to by purchasing individual accessories. A basic kit may include a handle applicator with interchangeable wool and sea sponge pads (A); a 3-compartment paint tray, for separating paints of different colors (B); a dual-roller with accented roller covers, for creating a blended two tone finish or a border (C); and edging and finishing tools, to complete designs in corners and small spaces (D).

Advanced Painting Materials

*L*atex and acrylic paints can be used successfully for a wide range of faux finishes and techniques. Because they are water-based, they are easy to clean up with just soap and water, and they are also safer for the environment than oil-based paints.

Water-based paints dry quickly, which is not necessarily an advantage in decorative painting, especially for techniques that re-quire some manipulation of the paint on the surface. To increase *open time,* or the length of time the paint can be manipulated, several paint additives have been devel-oped. These include latex paint conditioner, such as Floetrol, and acrylic paint extender. These products are available at paint retailers and craft supply stores.

For some decorative painting techniques, it is preferable to use a paint glaze, which is usu-ally thinner and more translucent than paint. There are some premixed acrylic paint glazes available in limited colors. These may be mixed to produce additional glaze colors. Untinted acrylic mediums in gloss, satin, or matte finishes also are available for mixing with acrylic or latex paint to make glazes. The glaze medium does not change the color of the paint; generally a small amount of paint is added to the glaze medium, just enough to give it the desired color. Latex or acrylic paint can also be mixed with water-based urethane or varnish for a very translucent glaze.

Tips for Using Paint Glazes

• Protect the surrounding area with a drop cloth or plastic sheet, and wear old clothing because working with a glaze can be messy.

• Use a wide painter's tape (page 84) to mask off the surrounding surfaces. Firmly rub the edges of the tape to ensure that the glaze will not seep under it.

• Use a paint roller to apply the glaze when even coverage is desired or when painting a large surface, such as a wall.

• Use a paintbrush to apply the glaze when smooth finish is desired, or when painting a small item.

• Use a sponge applicator to apply the glaze when more variation and pattern in the surface is desired, or when painting a small item.

• Manipulate glaze while it is still wet. Although humidity affects the setting time, the glaze can usually be manipulated for a few minutes.

• Work with an assistant when using glaze on a large surface. While one person applies the glaze, the other can manipulate it.

Low-luster latex enamel paint is used for the base coat under faux finishes. The slightly sheened surface gives the finish a base to cling to, while allowing manipulation tools to move easily on the surface.

Acrylic paints are available in a wide range of colors. They can be used alone for stenciling, or mixed with acrylic mediums to create glazes for decorative paint finishes.

Premixed acrylic paint glazes are available in a variety of colors for faux finishing. They are slightly translucent and contain additives for extended open time.

Acrylic mediums, or glaze mediums, can be mixed with acrylic or latex paint to create paint glazes with gloss, satin, or matte finishes.

Taped-off Designs

Simple techniques using painter's masking tape can help you create patterns like plaids, stripes, and other geometric designs. Select a professional-quality tape that prevents the paint from seeping underneath and can be removed easily without damaging the base coat. For best results, apply the paint in light coats, but take care not to thin the paint too much.

For stripes, use the painter's masking tape to divide the surface into parallel rows for precise painting. To create a plaid design, mask off and paint parallel rows, using one color at a time, first in one direction, then in the opposite direction.

How to Paint a Striped Design

2 Mark light plumb lines for the first stripe, using a pencil and a carpenter's level. Apply painter's masking tape along the lines, and press the edges firmly to ensure a good bond.

1 Apply a base coat in the desired color. Allow the paint to dry completely.

TOOLS & MATERIALS

- Carpenter's level
- Pencil
- Tape measure
- Small paint roller
- Paintbrush or paint roller, for base coat
- Latex or craft acrylic paints
- Painter's masking tape
- Sponge applicator

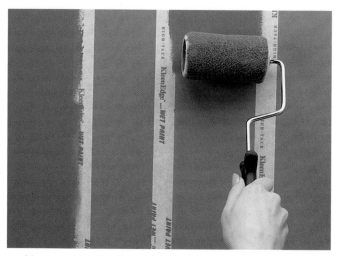

3 Measure from the first stripe, and draw parallel lines for the remaining stripes of the first color. Use the level to plumb each line. Apply the masking tape. Paint the stripes, using a paintbrush, small roller, or sponge applicator. Allow the paint to dry.

4 Remove the masking tape from the painted stripes. Repeat the process for any additional colors.

How to Paint a Plaid Design

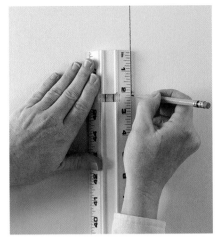

1 Apply a base coat of low-luster or mid-sheen latex enamel in the desired color. Allow the paint to dry. Measure and mark vertical plumb lines and horizontal level lines for the rows of the first paint color. Use a carpenter's level or bubble stick, and draw light pencil lines. Use a piece of plaid fabric as a guide for sizing and spacing the rows.

2 Apply painter's masking tape to the horizontal lines, pressing the tape firmly to seal the edges.

3 Thin the paint of the first color, using water, acrylic extender, or latex paint conditioner. The paint should be slightly translucent when applied. Paint the horizontal rows, using a sponge applicator. Pull the applicator from one end of the row to the other, making fine lines in the paint that simulate fabric weave. Allow the paint to dry, then remove the tape.

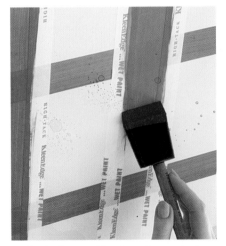

4 Apply the masking tape to create the vertical rows. Paint the vertical rows as with the horizontal rows, using the same color. Let the paint dry, then remove the tape.

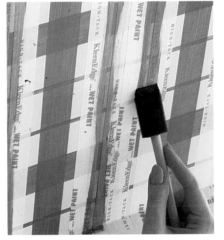

5 Mark lines for the horizontal and vertical rows of the next paint color. Repeat steps 2–4.

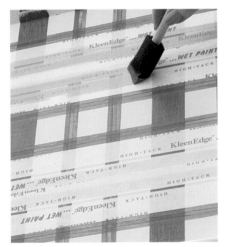

6 Repeat the process for the horizontal and vertical rows of each additional paint color.

TOOLS & MATERIALS

- Paintbrush or paint roller
- Tape measure
- Carpenter's level or bubble stick
- Pencil
- Sponge applicator

- Low-luster or mid-sheen latex enamel, for base coat
- Plaid fabric
- Painter's masking tape
- Latex or craft acrylic paints, for stripe colors

Freehand Designs

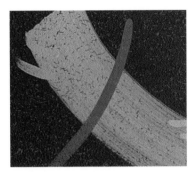

Swirls of paint created with sweeping brush strokes make interesting designs. The three easy-to-copy designs shown here and on page 170 are created primarily with basic painting tools, such as artist's brushes, texture rollers, and paint pads.

Paint the design on your walls rather than using wallcoverings, or paint fabrics for unique accent pillows instead of selecting patterned fabrics. For small accessories, use smaller brushes and shorter brush strokes.

Vary the paint colors, selecting different colors for the different brush strokes. Keep in mind that dark and dull colors tend to recede, while bright colors and metallic paints tend to advance. Metallic paints add drama by reflecting light. For painting on fabrics, use specialty paints designed for textiles.

When painting, overlap the brush strokes for a more layered, multi-dimensional look. Or, vary the spaces between the strokes for added interest. Before you begin the actual project, experiment with the paint colors and techniques by painting on a large sheet of cardboard or on a remnant of fabric.

TOOLS & MATERIALS

- #4 round artist's brush
- #4 fan brush
- #2 flat artist's brush
- 3" flat paintbrush
- Paint tray
- Texture roller
- Craft acrylic paints or fabric paints
- Paper towels

How to Paint a Small Swirled Design

1 Apply the first paint color to the sur-face in slightly curved brush strokes, using a #4 round artist's brush. Make the strokes about 4" long, spacing them 4" to 6" apart, Allow the paint to dry.

2 Apply the second color in curving brush strokes about 1½" long, using the same brush. Use less pressure on the brush so the strokes are not as wide as those of the first color. Allow some strokes to overlap those of the first color. Let the paint dry.

3 Apply the third color in curving strokes about 1" long, using the tip of the same brush. Allow some strokes to overlap those of the first color.

How to Paint a Medium Swirled Design

1 Apply the first paint color to the surface in brush strokes about 4" long, using a #4 fan brush. Allow the paint to dry.

2 Apply the second color through the middle of the first color in brush strokes about 6" long, using a #2 flat artist's brush. Vary the positions of the strokes for added interest. Allow the paint to dry.

3 Apply the third color in slightly curved strokes about 1½" to 2" long, using a #4 round artist's brush. Let the paint dry.

4 Wet the fan brush in water, and blot it on a paper towel. Separate the bristles into small fingers. Dip ¼" of the bristle tips into the fourth paint color, keeping the bristles separated. Paint the surface in short brush strokes, about 1" long, using light pressure.

How to Paint a Large Swirled Design

1 Dilute the first paint color, mixing one part paint to two parts water. Using a 3" paintbrush, apply the paint to the surface in slightly curved brush strokes, from 7" to 14" long. Allow the paint to dry.

2 Dilute the second paint color, mixing one part paint to one part water, and pour it into a paint tray. Dip a texture roller into the paint, then blot the roller onto paper. Roll the surface, overlapping the brush strokes from Step 1. Let the paint dry.

3 Apply the third color in curving brush strokes, about 6" to 12" long, using a #4 round artist's brush. Overlap the brush strokes from Step 1. Allow the paint to dry.

4 Apply the fourth color in pairs of short brush strokes, using a #4 round artist's brush. Overlap the edges of the strokes from Step 1.

Painting Advanced Designs & Finishes 171

Tips for Freehand Painting

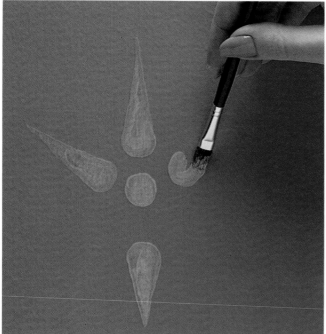

To create symmetrical motifs, paint the center of the design first. Then, paint the remaining elements of the design around the center. Start each element from the point closest to the center and work outward.

Use a tape measure and a carpenter's level or bubble stick to draw level reference marks for painting borders. Make light pencil marks at equal intervals to guide your freehand painting strokes. Keep the brush moving at a constant, rhythmic pace across the wall, redipping the brush in paint as necessary. Fill in any details after the entire border is laid out.

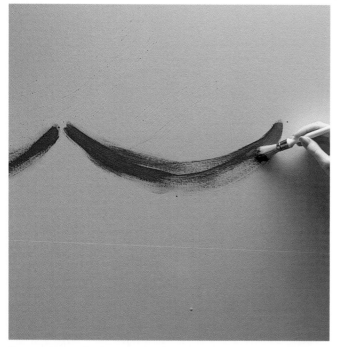

Draw a layout for large designs by marking faint pencil guidelines on the wall at strategic points. Paint the dominant details first to anchor the design's position on the wall. Then, complete the design by filling in the secondary details.

Random motifs can follow a less exact plan, but it helps to start with a rough layout to avoid an uneven distribution of designs. Before you begin painting, mark the placement for each motif, using a small piece of masking tape. Stand at a distance to get an overall view of the wall.

Freehand Design Variations

(Right) A contemporary asymmetrical design painted on the wall boldly outlines a window. Small motifs taken from the design are painted randomly on the wall, unifying the room.

(Below) A faux brickwork painted on the wall under a shelf resembles a fireplace and mantel. A faux brickwork chair rail continues around the room, drawing the eye toward the "fireplace" to make the room more intimate.

All-over Sponge Designs

*S*ponge painting produces a soft, mottled effect and is one of the easiest techniques to use. To achieve this paint finish, use a natural sea sponge to dab paint onto a surface. Do not use cellulose or synthetic sponges, because they tend to leave identical impressions with hard, defined edges.

The look of a sponge effect is determined by the number of paint colors applied, the sequence in which you apply the colors, and the distance between the sponge impressions. You can use semigloss, low-luster, or flat latex paint for the base coat and the sponging. Or, for a translucent finish, use a paint glaze that consists of paint, paint conditioner, and water; mix them according to the instructions on page 176.

To create stripes, borders, or panels, use painter's masking tape to mask off the desired areas of the surface after you apply the first color of sponged paint. Then, apply another color to the unmasked areas.

To sponge paint fabric, use fabric paint or craft acrylic paint mixed with textile medium. Prewash the fabric to remove any sizing, if the fabric is washable, and press it well to remove any wrinkles. Apply the paint with a sea sponge, as in Step 2, page 176, but do not blot it with a wet sponge. When the fabric is dry, heat-set the paint, using a dry iron and a press cloth.

How to Sponge Paint

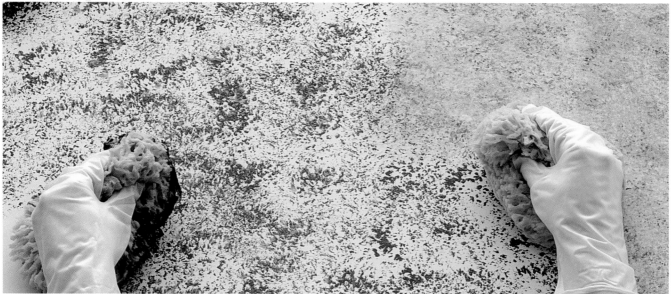

1 Apply a base coat of latex or acrylic paint. Allow the paint to dry. Rinse a sea sponge in water to soften it, then squeeze out most of the water. Saturate the sponge with paint or paint glaze (page 162). Blot the sponge lightly onto a paper towel. Press the sponge repeatedly onto the surface. Work quickly in small areas, and change the position of the sponge often. Using a wet sea sponge held in your other hand, blot the applied paint immediately, as shown. This causes the paint to bleed, for a softened, blended look. Some of the paint will be removed by the wet sponge.

2 Continue to apply the first paint color to the project area, blotting with the moist sponge. Repeat the technique, using one or more additional colors of paint, if desired. Allow the paint to dry between applications.

3 To create a feathered effect, apply the final paint color using a light, sweeping motion instead of dabbing.

TOOLS & MATERIALS

- Paintbrush or paint roller, for base coat
- Natural sea sponges
- Carpenter's level
- Pencil
- Ruler
- Craft acrylic or latex paints
- Latex paint conditioner and water, for glaze
- Painter's masking tape

SPONGING GLAZE

Mix together the following ingredients:
1 part latex or craft acrylic paint
1 part latex paint conditioner
1 part water

How to Sponge Paint Stripes, Borders, or Panels

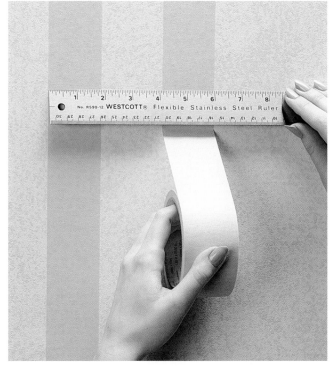

1 Complete Steps 1 to 3 on page 176. Allow the paint to dry thoroughly. Mark a light plumb line, using a pencil and carpenter's level. Position the first row of painter's masking tape along this line. Use a ruler to measure and position remaining rows of masking tape to establish stripes, borders, or panel areas.

2 Apply a second paint color to the un-masked areas of the surface. Blot or feather the paint, as desired. Allow the paint to dry. Carefully remove the masking tape.

Sponging Variations

To achieve a harmonious look, use related colors for sponge painting, such as two warm colors or two cool colors. For a bolder and more unexpected look, sponge paint with a combination of warm and cool colors.

Warm and cool colors, like yellow and blue, combine boldly, but sponge painting softens the effect.

Cool colors, like green and blue, blend together for a tranquil effect.

Warm colors, like yellow and orange, blend together for an exciting effect.

Terra-Cotta Finish

*I*nstantly warm up any room by painting the walls with a terra-cotta finish. Terra-cotta was once considered a complicated design that required a professional faux finish painter. However, with tools such as the Wagner Faux Magic Wool Pad, you can easily create this design, regardless of your skill level. Unlike many other faux finishes, a terra-cotta finish does not require a preliminary base coat. Using a wool pad, apply colors to the surface, and blend them together. The more you blend the paints, the more muted the finish becomes. Faux finish kits and wool pads are available at paint retailers and home stores.

The terra-cotta finish shown here was created with three shades of latex paint: deep brown, dark clay, and apricot. The overall hue of your design will depend on the colors you choose. For a rosier terra-cotta finish, select colors with a red base. Or, if you prefer a finish with an orange overtone, select colors with a yellow base. If you're not certain which colors to choose, your paint retailer can help you find the right combination.

How to Produce a Terra-Cotta Finish with a Wool Pad

- Divided paint tray
- Paint stirrer sticks
- Wool paint pad
- Wool finishing tool
- Brown, clay, and apricot latex paint
- Paint glaze

1 Pour each shade of paint into a separate section of a divided paint tray. Add ¼ cup of paint glaze (page 163) to each color, blending it into the paint with a paint stirrer stick. Season the wool pad by wetting your hand with water and running it over the wool to remove lint and loose fibers.

2 Dip the wool pad into the brown paint, and scrape the pad along the edge of the tray to remove excess paint. Working in 4' × 4' sections, apply the paint by pressing the pad to the wall in a random pattern. Cover about 80% of the wall surface in each section, leaving some bare spots visible.

3 Scrape the pad to remove as much of the brown paint from the pad as possible. You do not need to wash the pad before applying the next paint color.

4 Dip the wool pad into the clay paint, and scrape off the excess. Using the same stamping technique you used to apply the brown paint, fill in the bare spots in the section with the clay paint. When you are finished, scrape the clay paint from the pad, as before.

5 Dip the wool pad into the apricot paint, and remove the excess. Using the random stamping technique, lightly press the wool pad onto the painted section. You will begin to see the paint blend. The more you apply the apricot paint, the more the paint will blend and the lighter the final design will be.

6 Once you've finished the 4' × 4' section, use a wool edging tool to paint the design into any corners and at the edges of the section. Season the wool tool, as with the wool pad. Repeat steps 2 through 5, applying the brown, clay, and apricot paints, blending until the design is complete. When you are done with the section, move on to the next section and repeat the process.

Wool Pad Variations

You can use your wool pad for a variety of finishes. Follow the same stamping technique used to create the terra-cotta finish, and combine two or more colors for a custom design. A basic tone-on-tone finish requires only two colors of different shades.

Tone-on-Tone: Select two paints that are three or four colors apart on a monochromatic paint selection strip, one in a dark shade and one in a light shade. Apply the dark color first. Using the random stamping technique, cover nearly all of the 4' × 4' section. Then, apply the lighter color, stamping it in until the paints are blended to create the desired effect.

Contrasting Tones: Combine a contrasting color with two shades of the same color for a bold, eye-catching pattern. Apply the same-color shades first, starting with the darker shade, then the lighter. Apply the contrasting shade last, taking care not to blend it too much. If you over-blend, the colors will become muddy and you'll loose the effect of the contrasting shade.

Metallic Accent: Create a striking design by using the wool pad to apply a metallic glaze over a tone-on-tone finish. Begin by painting a tone on tone finish. Use another clean wool pad to lightly tap on a metallic glaze with a quick stamping motion. If you stamp too much, you'll over-blend the glaze and loose the effect.

Check Pattern Sponge Design

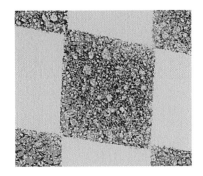

*F*or a dramatic check pattern on walls, apply paint with squares of cellulose sponge. Start by constructing a simple stamp applicator, using a glue gun and a small piece of plywood. Paint the checks in one or more colors, following a simple layout. If desired, you can add more dimension and color to the design by lightly stamping additional paint colors over the checks. Use a square stamp of the same size, or make a smaller stamp with a different shape to apply accent colors.

A check pattern with even rows works best with walls that have square corners and level ceiling lines. Start painting at the most prominent corner of the room, and work in both directions from that point, so that full squares will meet at that corner. If the room has no conspicuous corners, start in the center of the most prominent wall, dividing the layout evenly into checks across the width of the wall.

Use flat latex or low-luster latex enamel paint for painting walls. To provide a more durable, washable finish on cabinets and furniture, use a gloss enamel.

How to Sponge Paint a Check Design

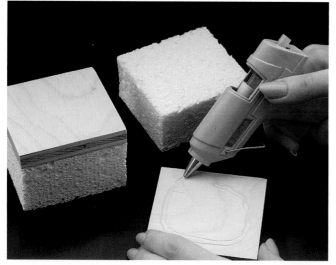

1 Cut the sponge into the desired size of square. Cut the plywood to match the sponge. Secure the sponge to the plywood with hot glue. Make one stamp for each color and shape in the design.

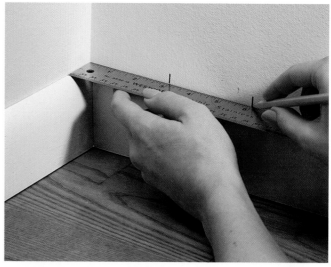

2 Apply a base coat of paint to the wall in the desired background color, and allow the paint to dry. Lay out the placement of the first row of checks at bottom of the wall, using a ruler and pencil. Mark the wall at intervals equal to the width of the stamp. For example, if you have a 3" square stamp, mark the wall every 3".

TOOLS & MATERIALS

- Hot glue gun and glue sticks
- Carpenter's level
- Pencil
- Ruler

- Saw
- Latex paints
- Large cellulose sponges
- Scraps of ¼" plywood
- Thin, transparent Mylar sheets

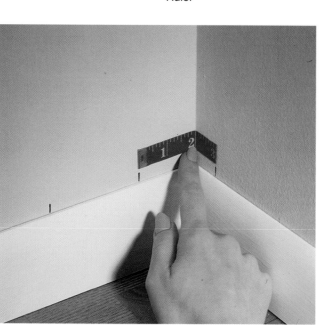

3 If you reach the end of the wall and the full width of the design does not fit into the corner, continue the measurement around the corner, and mark the edges of the design on both walls. Then, continue marking full widths on the new wall. A fabric measuring tape makes it easy to measure around corners.

4 Mark a plumb line at the first mark from the starting corner, using a carpenter's level and pencil. Continue the line up the wall, and draw lightly so the pencil line will not show through the paint. For a more accurate layout, mark an additional plumb line every few rows.

5 Apply paint to the sponge, using a paintbrush. Stamp the bottom row of checks onto the wall.

6 Continue to stamp rows of checks, working up from the bottom of the wall and using the preceding row and plumb line as horizontal and vertical guides. If the full stamped design does not fit into corners or at the top of the wall, leave the area unpainted at this time.

7 Allow the paint to dry. To fill in the areas left unstamped, place a piece of Mylar over the painted checks to protect the wall. Stamp the design up to the corners or top of the wall, overlapping the stamp onto the Mylar. Let the paint dry.

8 Apply another paint color, if desired, stamping very lightly over the painted checks.

Block-printed Designs

*B*lock printing is a simple stamping technique used to apply repeated motifs to walls. With this technique, you apply paint to a printing block, using a paint-saturated felt pad, then stamp the block onto the wall surface. You can arrange the block prints to form a border or a set pattern, or you can scatter them randomly across a surface.

Manufactured print blocks can be purchased in a variety of sizes and designs. For a more personal decorative touch, make your own printing block, using closed-cell foam secured to a wood block. Closed-cell foam is a good material for making print blocks because it is easy to cut and it has the flexibility to make clean prints, even on somewhat irregular wall surfaces.

Closed-cell foam is manufactured in several forms. Thin, self-adhesive foam sheets are available at art supply stores. Use scissors to cut these into the desired shapes. Another type of closed-cell foam is neoprene, a synthetic rubber manufactured for use as an insulator. It is commonly available for use as weatherstripping, in a ⅜"-thick, self-adhesive tape; however, the widest tape available in this form is ¾". To find neoprene in sheet form, look for suppliers listed in the Yellow Pages under Foam. You can also use an old computer mouse pad made of neoprene, although the surface may be textured.

Use acrylic craft paints for block printing on walls. Make a stamp pad for transferring the paint to the printing block by soaking a piece of felt with the paint. To increase the "open" time of the paint and keep the stamp pad moist longer, make a glaze by mixing the paint with a small amount of latex paint conditioner. It's a good idea to practice using the printing block on paper before printing on the wall, to become familiar with the placement of the design in relation to the outer edge of the block.

How to Make a Printing Block

TOOLS & MATERIALS

- Pencil
- Scissors
- Small artist's brush or sponge
- Tracing paper
- Wood block
- Closed-cell foam
- Graphite paper
- Craft glue
- Masking tape or pencil
- Craft acrylic paints and acrylic paint extender
- Felt
- Glass or acrylic sheet

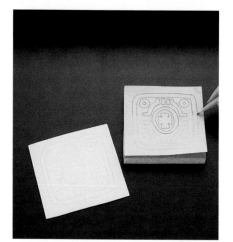

1 Cut the tracing paper to the same size as the wood block, and draw the design onto the paper. Mark the top of the design on the paper and block. Transfer the design onto the back of the closed-cell foam, using graphite paper. Then, transfer the image to the face of the wood block.

2 Cut the foam along the design lines, using scissors. Peel off the paper backing and affix the foam pieces to the block, following the transferred design lines. If you are using foam that is not self-adhesive, use craft glue to secure it to the block.

3 Glue the original pattern on the back side of the block, taking care to position it in the same direction as the design on the face of the block.

How to Block-print a Design on a Wall

1 Mark the placement for the design motifs on the wall, using masking tape or light pencil lines. Thin the paint slightly with an acrylic paint extender, mixing about three to four parts paint to one part extender.

2 Cut a piece of felt larger than the printing block and place it on a sheet of glass or acrylic. Pour the paint mixture onto the felt pad, allowing it to saturate the fabric.

3 Press the printing block into the felt pad, coating the surface of the foam evenly with paint.

4 Press the printing block to the wall at the placement mark, applying firm, even pressure to the back of the block. Remove the block by pulling it straight back from the wall.

5 Repeat steps 2 and 3 for each block print. Add paint to the felt pad as needed. Touch up any poor impressions, using a small artist's brush, sponge, or piece of foam.

Stenciled Designs

*U*se stenciled motifs to highlight an area of a room or to simulate architectural details, such as chair rails. A variety of precut stencils is available in a wide range of prices, which usually are determined by the intricacy of the design. Or, you can make custom stencils by tracing designs onto transparent Mylar sheets. For stencils that coordinate with home furnishings, adapt a design from wallpaper, fabric, or artwork. Use a photocopy machine to enlarge or reduce patterns to the desired size.

Most precut stencils will have a separate plate for each color and will be numbered according to the sequence for use. A single stencil plate may be used for multiple colors if the spaces between the design areas are large enough to be covered with masking tape. When stenciling multicolored designs, apply the largest part of the design first. When stenciling borders, it is generally best to apply all the repeats of the first color before applying the second color.

Before starting a project, carefully plan the placement of the design. Stencil the design onto paper, and tape it to the surface to check the design placement. Border designs with obvious repeats, such as swags or bows, require careful planning to avoid any partial motifs. If you are stenciling a border, the placement may be influenced by the position of room details, such as windows, doors, and heating vents. It is generally best to start at the most prominent area and work outward. The spacing between border repeats may be altered slightly, if necessary.

Use high-quality stiff stencil brushes in sizes proportionate to the space being stenciled. Use a separate brush for each color, or clean the brush and allow it to dry before reusing it.

For painting hard surfaces, such as walls and woodwork, use craft acrylic paint or oil-based stencil paint in liquid or solid form. You may stencil over a clean, painted surface or over finished wood. If the surface is finished wood, apply a clear finish or sealer to the entire surface after it is stenciled.

For stenciling on fabric, use fabric paints or combine two parts craft acrylic paint to one part textile medium. Neither type of paint will cause the fabric to stiffen. Follow the manufacturer's directions to heat-set the paints. For good penetration of the paint, select fabric that is at least 50% cotton. Avoid fabrics with polished or protective finishes, and prewash fabrics to remove any sizing.

How to Make a Custom Stencil

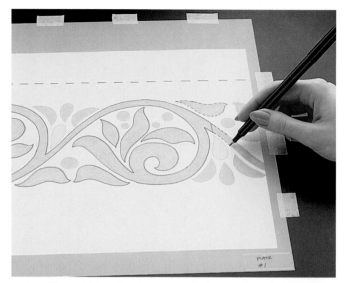

1 Draw or trace the design onto a sheet of paper. Repeat the design, if necessary, so it is 13" to 18" long, making sure the spacing between repeats is consistent. Color the design, using colored pencils. Mark placement lines to help you position the stencil on the wall.

2 Position a Mylar sheet over the design so the edges of the sheet extend beyond the top and bottom of the design by at least 1". Secure the sheet with masking tape. Trace the areas that will be stenciled in the first color, using a marking pen. Transfer the placement lines.

3 Trace the design areas for each additional color onto a separate Mylar sheet. To help you align the stencil, outline the areas for previous colors with dotted lines. Layer all of the Mylar sheets, and check for accuracy. Using a mat knife and straightedge, trim the outer edges of the stencil plates, leaving a 1" to 3" border around the design.

TOOLS & MATERIALS

- Paper
- Colored pencils
- Transparent Mylar sheets
- Masking tape
- Fine-point permanent-ink marking pen
- Cutting surface, such as a self-healing cutting board or cardboard
- Mat knife
- Metal ruler

4 Separate the Mylar sheets. Cut out the traced areas on each sheet, using a mat knife. Cut the smallest shapes first, then cut the larger ones. Pull the knife toward you as you cut, turning the Mylar sheet, rather than the knife, to change the cutting direction.

How to Stencil on Hard Surfaces

TOOLS & MATERIALS

- Carpenter's level and pencil
- Stencil brushes
- Artist's brush
- Precut or custom stencil
- Masking tape
- Spray adhesive, optional
- Craft acrylic paints, or liquid or solid oil-based stencil paints
- Clear wood finish and paintbrush, if stenciling on wood
- Disposable plates
- Paper towels

1 Mark the placement for the stencil on the surface with masking tape. Or, draw a light reference line, using a carpenter's level and a pencil. Position the stencil plate for the first color, aligning the placement line with the tape or pencil line. Secure the stencil in place, using masking tape or spray adhesive.

Stenciling Variation

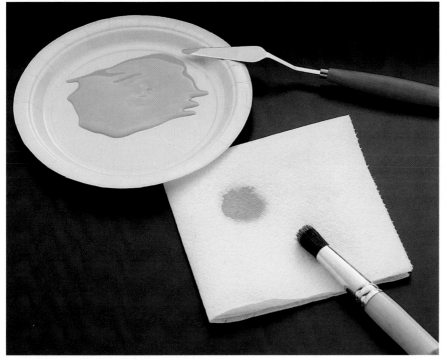

2 Place 1 to 2 tsp. of acrylic or oil-based paint on a disposable plate. Dip the tip of a stencil brush into the paint. Blot the brush onto a folded paper towel, using a circular motion, until the bristles are almost dry.

To stencil with solid paint, or crayon paint, remove the protective coating from the crayon tip, using a paper towel. Rub a 1½" circle of paint onto a blank area of the stencil. Load a stencil brush by lightly rubbing the brush over the paint in a circular motion, first in one direction, then in the other direction.

(continued next page)

3 Hold the brush perpendicular to the surface. Apply the paint within the cut areas of the stencil, using a circular motion. Stencil all of the cut areas of the first stencil plate, and allow the paint to dry. Remove the stencil.

4 Secure the second plate to the surface, matching the design. Apply the second paint color in all of the cut areas. Repeat the process for any remaining stencils and colors until the design is completed.

Stenciling Variation:

5 After all of the paints are completely dry, touch up any glitches or smudges on the surface, using background paint and an artist's brush.

While the circular method of stenciling results in a blended finish, the stippling method produces a deeper, textured appearance. To stipple, wrap masking tape around the bristles of a stenciling brush, ¼" from the ends. Hold the brush perpendicular to the surface, and apply the paint using a dabbing motion. This method is also used to stencil fabric.

Techniques for Shaded Designs

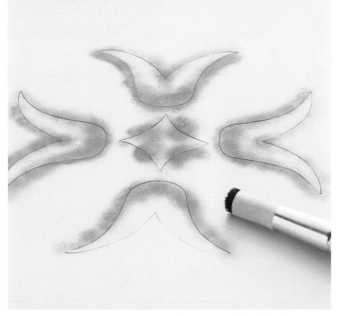

Apply paint within the cut areas of the stencil, leaving the centers lighter than the edges. For an aged, fade-away effect, use a heavier touch at the base of the motif and a lighter touch at the top.

Apply a complementary or darker color of paint, shading the outer edges of the cut areas.

Apply paint to the outer edges of the cut areas and allow it to dry. Hold a piece of Mylar in place to cover a portion of the area, and apply paint next to the edge of the Mylar. For example, cover one-half of a leaf to stencil the veins.

Tip:

Clean stencil brushes used to apply acrylic paints by applying a small amount of dishwashing detergent to the brush. Rub the bristles in the palm of your hand in a circular motion until all of the paint is removed. Rinse with water and allow the bristles to dry. To remove oil-based paint, first clean the brush with mineral spirits and dry it on paper towels. Then, wash the brush with detergent and rinse with water.

Trompe l'Oeil Stenciled Designs

For people who are less confident of their freehand painting skills or would simply like to try another avenue, a trompe l'oeil effect can be created with stencils. There are some high-quality precut stencils available, with multiple overlays that help you create realistic, life-size images. By using shading and highlighting techniques, you can add depth and perspective, giving the stenciled images visual dimension.

Better, more realistic stencils do not have the bridges, or blank spaces, found on less expensive stencils. Better stencils also have pinpoint registration marks to ensure that each overlay lines up exactly over the preceding one. A wide selection of stencil brushes allows you to use a different brush for each paint color, in sizes proportionate to the sizes of the stencil openings. Using craft acrylic paints and a pouncing method of application allows for successful blending of colors and shading. Wrap masking tape around the bristles, 1/4" from the ends, to help support the bristles during the pouncing motion.

Follow the manufacturer's instructions and color suggestions for completing the stencil, or select your own color combinations. Several colors may be applied with each overlay, depending on the complexity of the design. Each opening may receive a base color, applied in gradation shading, and then another color for darker shading in areas that would appear in shadow. As with other trompe l'oeil methods, you should determine an imaginary light source, highlighting foreground areas that would be in direct line with that light source, and shading areas that would appear in shadow. After completing the stenciled image, fill in the "shadows."

TOOLS & MATERIALS

- Precut stencil with multiple overlays
- Painter's masking tape
- Stencil brushes
- Disposable plates
- Paper towels
- Masking tape
- Pencil
- Craft acrylic paints

How to Stencil a Trompe l'Oeil Design

1 Position the first overlay as desired, and secure it in place, with painter's masking tape. Mark the surface through the registration holes, using a sharp pencil.

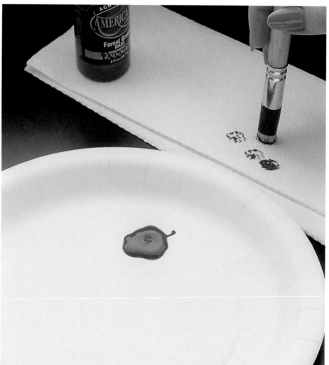

2 Pour 1 to 2 tsp. of paint onto a plate. Wrap masking tape around the bristles of a stenciling brush, ¼" from the ends. Dip the brush tip into the paint. Using a circular motion, blot the brush onto a paper towel until the bristles are almost dry.

3 Hold the brush perpendicular to the surface, and apply the paint to the first opening, using an up-and-down pouncing motion. Paint lightly and evenly over the entire opening.

4 Deepen the color in the areas of the opening that would appear in shadow, by repeated pouncing. Leave highlighted areas more pale.

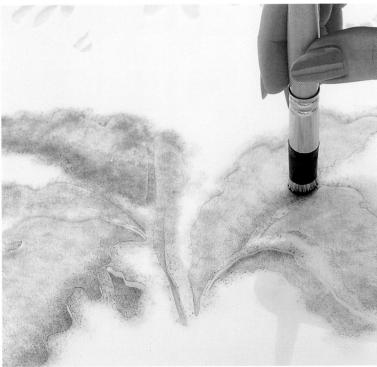

5 Repeat steps 3 and 4 for all openings that receive the same color. Repeat step 2, using the shading color and another brush. Apply shading to areas of the openings that would appear in shadow.

6 Repeat Steps 2 to 5 for any additional colors on the first overlay. Remove the overlay.

7 Position the second overlay by aligning the registration marks, and tape it in place. Repeat steps 2 to 6 for the second overlay. Repeat for any subsequent overlays until the image is complete.

8 Follow step 2, using a small stencil brush and gray or brown paint. Apply the paint lightly with a pouncing motion along the edges of image opposite the light source, to simulate shadows.

Scumbled Wall Designs

Scumbling is a simple painting technique you can use to create textural geometric patterns that mimic the look of expensive wallcovering. With this technique, a large stencil brush is used to dry-brush paint onto the wall in swirling motions over a base coat. Because very little paint is required for dry-brushing, small jars of acrylic craft paints can be used. Choose two or three related decorator colors. Or, for a look that is classic and rich, use gold and silver metallic paints.

You can customize the geometric design, covering an entire wall, as shown in the diamond design on the opposite page. Or plan a chair rail in a block pattern, a ceiling border made of triangular shapes, or a striped wainscoting. Use painter's masking tape to mask off the designs.

Measure each wall, and sketch the geometric design on graph paper to help you determine the scale and placement of the design. Before painting the walls, experiment with the painting technique, making test samples on sheets of cardboard.

To prepare the surface, clean the walls, removing any dirt or grease, and rinse them with clear water. If the walls are unfinished, apply a primer and allow it to dry thoroughly before applying the masking tape.

TOOLS & MATERIALS

- Ruler
- Pencil
- Paint roller
- Carpenter's level
- Straightedge
- Putty knife
- Stencil brush, 1" in diameter
- Graph paper
- Painter's masking tape
- Latex paint, for base coat
- Latex or craft acrylic paints, for scumbling
- Disposable plates
- Paper towels

How to Paint a Taped-Off Scumbled Design

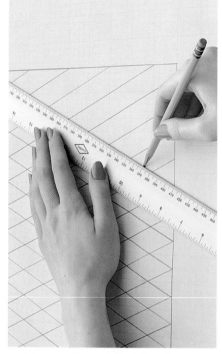

1 Measure the wall, and plan the design to scale on graph paper. Apply a base coat of paint, using a paint roller.

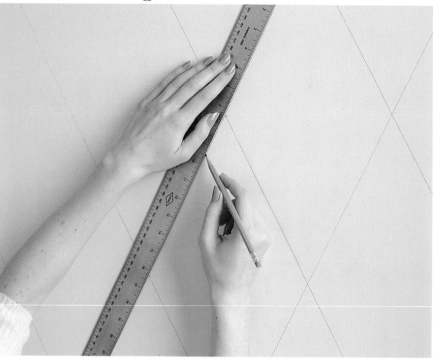

2 Allow the paint to dry. Draw the design on the wall with pencil, using a straight-edge as a guide.

3 Mark the sections that will be masked off. Apply painter's masking tape to the marked sections, using a putty knife to trim the tape diagonally at the corners. Press along all edges of the tape, using a plastic credit card or your fingernail to create a tight seal.

4 Pour a small amount of each paint color onto a disposable plate. Dip the tip of the stencil brush into the first color. Using a circular motion, blot the brush onto a paper towel until the bristles are almost dry.

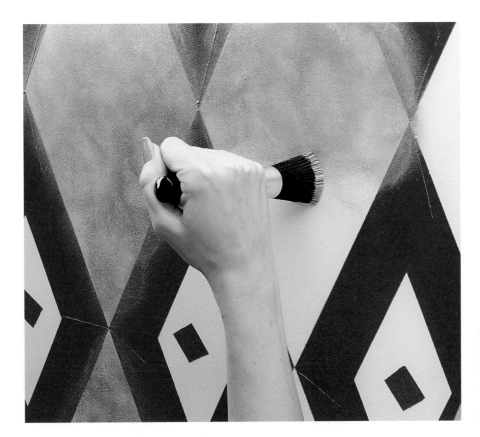

5 Brush the paint onto the wall with vigorous, wide, circular motions. Work in a small area at a time, and change the direction of the circular motions frequently. Overlap the paint onto the masking tape. Build up the color to the desired intensity, but allow the base coat to show through. Use all of the paint on bristles before applying more.

6 Dip the brush into the second color, and blot the brush. Apply the paint randomly over the same area, building up the color to varying intensities throughout the area. Repeat with a third color, if desired.

7 Repeat the technique to complete the entire wall, working in one small area at a time and blending areas together. Remove the masking tape when the paint is dry.

Stained Floor Finishes

Stains are applied to the surface of unfinished wood floors to change the color of the wood. Colored stains can also be applied to previously stained and finished floors for a colorwashed effect. Look for a water-based stain that is formulated for easy application without lap marks or streaking. Use a wood conditioner on the wood prior to staining, if recommended by the manufacturer. Conditioners can help prevent streaking and help control grain raise when using water-based wood stains. Stains are available in a variety of natural wood tones. Or select a colored stain, such as green for a country decorating scheme, or white for a contemporary look.

You can also stain wood by colorwashing it with diluted latex paint. The colorwash solution will be considerably lighter in color than the original paint color. Use the formula on page 207 to make a color-wash solution, and experiment with small amounts of paint until you achieve the desired color. Apply the stain or colorwash solution in an inconspicuous area, such as a closet, to test the application method and color before staining the entire floor surface. Protect the stained floor by sealing it with three coats of clear finish in satin, semi-gloss, or gloss. Choose a finish that is self-leveling to prevent brush marks.

TOOLS & MATERIALS

- Rubber gloves
- Synthetic brush, sponge applicator, or cotton lint-free rag, for applying stain
- Sponge applicator or paint pad and pole extension, for applying clear finish
- Power sander, fine sandpaper
- Wood conditioner, optional

- Tack cloth
- Cotton lint-free rags, for wiping stain
- Water-based stain or latex paint in desired color
- High-gloss and satin clear finishes, such as acrylic or polyurethane, for protecting stained floor

How to Apply a Stained Finish to a Bare Wood Floor

1 Sand the floor surface, using fine-grit sandpaper, sanding in the direction of the wood grain. Remove the sanding dust with a vacuum, then wipe the floor with a tack cloth.

2 Wear rubber gloves for working with any stain product. Stir the stain or colorwash solution thoroughly. Apply the stain or solution to the floor, using a synthetic brush or a sponge applicator. Work in small sections at a time. Keep a wet edge on the brush or applicator, and avoid overlapping the brush strokes.

3 Wipe away excess stain immediately, or after the waiting time recommended by the manufacturer, using a dry lint-free rag; wipe against the grain of the wood first, then wipe with the grain. Continue applying and wiping the stain until the entire floor is finished. Allow the stain to dry. Sand the floor lightly, using fine-grit sandpaper, then remove any sanding dust with a tack cloth. For a deeper color, apply a second coat of stain, and allow it to dry thoroughly.

4 Apply a coat of high-gloss clear finish to the stained floor, using a sponge applicator or a paint pad with a pole extension. Allow the finish to dry. Sand the floor lightly, using fine-grit sandpaper, then wipe with a tack cloth. Apply two coats of satin clear finish.

Wood Stain Variations

Dark wood tones work well for traditional rooms. White colorwashing over a previously dark stained floor mellows the formal appearance.

FLOOR COLORWASH SOLUTION

Mix together the following ingredients:
    1 part latex paint
    4 parts water

Medium, warm wood tones have a casual appearance. White colorwashing over a medium wood tone creates an antiqued look.

Pale neutral stains often are used for contemporary rooms. A blue colorwash can give a pale floor a bold new character.

Overall Painted Checkerboard Floor Design

*P*ainted designs in a variety of styles can be applied to wood floors to give the entire floor a new look or to accent certain areas. If the floor is in poor condition, it can be camouflaged with an all-over design, such as a classic checkerboard pattern.

Proper preparation of the floor is essential to give long-lasting results. For a previously finished wood floor, lightly sand the areas to be painted, so the paint will adhere well to the finish. For an unfinished wood floor, prevent the paint from penetrating the grain of the bare wood by sealing it with a clear acrylic or polyurethane finish and sanding it lightly before it is painted. Be sure that the floor is free of dust before you start to paint.

Plan the design on graph paper, and transfer it to the floor. Use painter's masking tape to mask off the lines for the checkerboard design. After painting the design, apply several coats of clear finish to the entire floor.

TOOLS & MATERIALS

- Power sander and fine-grit sandpaper
- Paintbrushes
- Tape measure
- Straightedge
- Pencil
- Paint roller, or paint pad and pole extension, for applying clear finish

- Graph paper
- Tack cloth
- Painter's masking tape
- Latex paint in the two desired colors and sheen
- High-gloss and satin clear finishes, such as acrylic or polyurethane

How to Paint an Overall Checkerboard Design on a Wood Floor

1 Degloss the finish of a previously stained and sealed wood floor by sanding the surface lightly, using a power sander and fine-grit sandpaper. This improves the paint adhesion. Vacuum the entire floor, then wipe it with a tack cloth to remove all sanding dust.

2 Mask off the baseboards with painter's masking tape. Paint the entire floor with the lighter of the two paint colors. Allow the paint to dry thoroughly.

3 Measure the floor and determine the size of squares you will use. Plan the design so that the areas of the floor with the highest visibility, such as the main entrance, have full squares. Place partial squares along walls in less conspicuous areas. Mark the design lines on the floor, using a straightedge and a pencil.

4 Mask off the squares that are to remain light in color, using painter's masking tape. Press firmly along all edges of the tape, using a plastic credit card or your fingernail to create a tight seal.

5 Paint the remaining squares with the darker paint color. Paint in small areas at a time, and remove the masking tape from painted squares before the paint is completely dry.

6 After all of the paint has dried completely, apply a coat of high-gloss clear finish, using a paint roller or paint pad with a pole extension. Allow the finish to dry. Sand the finish lightly with fine-grit sandpaper, then wipe the floor with a tack cloth. Apply two coats of satin clear finish.

Aged & Distressed Floor Finishes

A ged finishes give floors timeworn character, making them especially suitable for a country or informal decorating scheme. Though they appear distressed and fragile, these finishes are actually very durable.

Aged finishes are especially suitable for previously painted or stained floors, but may also be applied to new or resurfaced wood flooring. Up to three coats of paint in different colors may be applied to the floor. As the floor is sanded, varying amounts of the different colors are revealed, creating the illusion that the floor had been painted different colors over time. Additional wear and stress can be simulated by pounding the floor with a hammer, chisel, or chain. Two coats of clear finish are applied to protect the distressed finish.

For previously stained and finished floors, the existing finish can also be used as the base coat. Sanding will then reveal areas of stained wood under the paint. To achieve the same look on new or resurfaced wood flooring, first stain the wood, as shown on page 206 (steps 2 to 4), omitting only the satin finish coats.

The paint colors can be selected to complement each other and blend with the desired color scheme of the room. The top coat will be the most prominent, while the undercoats will show only in small amounts in the finished floor. For best results, select contrasting colors for the paint layers.

TOOLS & MATERIALS

- Paint roller
- Power sander, medium- and fine-grit sandpaper
- Hammer, chisel, chain, and awl, for distressing floor
- Latex enamel paints
- Satin clear finish
- Tack cloth

Tips For Preparing & Painting Wood Flooring

• Apply stain-killing primer over any knotholes in new or resurfaced wood. This seals the wood and prevents the paint from yellowing.

• Apply clear acrylic sealer to new or resurfaced wood to prevent paint from penetrating the grain of the bare wood.

• Clean previously painted floors with TSP (trisodium phosphate) to remove any wax, grease, or oil. Rinse the floor with clear water and allow it to dry.

• Sand a finished floor in the direction of the wood grain, using fine-grit sandpaper. Vacuum the floor thoroughly, then wipe it with a tack cloth to remove dust.

• Apply two or three coats of latex enamel floor paint, using a roller, paintbrush, or sponge applicator. Allow the paint to dry thoroughly between coats. Sand the floor lightly between coats, using fine-grit sandpaper. Wipe the floor with tack cloth before painting.

How to Apply an Aged and Distressed Finish to a Wood Floor

Although the goal of distressing your wood floor is to make it appear old and worn, you don't want to leave the wood unprotected. Moisture can ruin floor boards and damage the floor's structural supports. Once you have completed the distressed finish, apply two coats of satin clear finish over the entire floor, using a paint roller or a paint pad with a pole extension. Sand the finish lightly between coats, and wipe the floor with a tack cloth to remove dust.

1 Follow the tips above for a finish with a painted base coat. Or, for finish with a stained base coat, follow steps 2 to 4 on page 206, omitting the satin finish. Apply two or three coats of enamel, using a different color of paint for each coat.

2 Sand the floor surface with medium-grit sandpaper, sanding harder in some areas to remove the top and middle coats of paint. Avoid sanding beyond the base coat of paint or stain.

3 Distress the floor further, if desired, by hitting the wood with the head of a hammer or a chain. Gouge the boards with a chisel, or pound holes randomly, using an awl. Create as many imperfections as desired, then sand the floor lightly with fine-grit sandpaper.

Color Effect Variations

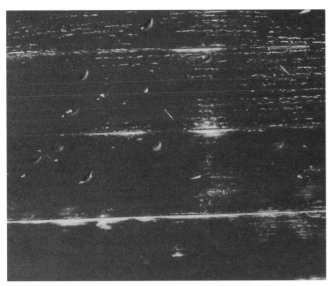

Here, two coats of dark green paint were applied over a previously stained floor. Sanding revealed the stain in some areas. The floor was further distressed using a hammer, chisel, and awl.

This finish was created with a maroon base coat and light rose top coat painted over a previously stained floor. Sanding revealed all three layers.

Strié & Combed Finishes

Strié and combed finishes are created by similar techniques in which a tool is dragged over wet glaze to reveal a base coat of a different color. The result is a textured, linear pattern, which can run in vertical lines, curves, swirls, zig-zags, or a weave pattern resembling fabric. Both finishes start with a base coat of low-luster latex enamel, followed by a latex or acrylic glaze mixture. The differences between these finishes are the result of the tools used to create the pattern.

The strié effect is created using a dry, natural-bristle brush, resulting in fine, irregular streaks and an interesting blend of color variations. A combed finish can be made with a variety of specialty tools, offering a range of patterns and designs. An additional option for the combed finish is to use a thickened glaze, which gives an opaque look and more distinct lines and texture.

Since the glaze must be wet for brushing or combing, timing is important with both techniques. For large surfaces, it is helpful to work with an assistant. After one person has applied the glaze, the other person brushes or combs through the glaze before it dries. If you are working alone, limit yourself to smaller sections. For best results, practice the technique and experiment with different glaze thicknesses by testing the finish on mat board before painting the wall.

TOOLS & MATERIALS

- Paint roller or natural-bristle paintbrush
- Wide natural-bristle brush
- Soft natural-bristle paintbrush
- Combing tool
- Low-luster latex enamel, for base coat
- Latex paint in desired sheen and color, for glaze
- Latex paint conditioner, such as Floetrol
- Rags

BASIC GLAZE
Mix together the following ingredients:
   1 part latex or craft acrylic paint
   1 part latex paint conditioner
   1 part water

THICKENED GLAZE
Mix together the following ingredients:
   2 parts latex or craft acrylic paint
   1 part acrylic paint thickener (may be used with latex paints)

How to Apply a Strié Paint Finish

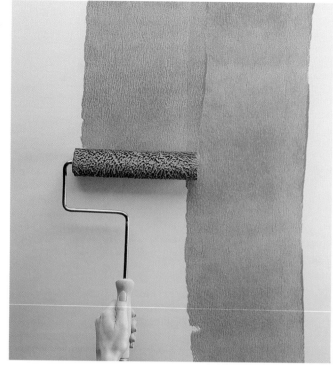

1 Apply the base coat of low-luster latex enamel, and allow the paint to dry. Mix the glaze (page 217). Apply the glaze over the base coat in a vertical section about 18" wide, using a paint roller or natural-bristle paintbrush.

2 Drag a dry, wide natural-bristle brush through the wet glaze, immediately after the glaze is applied; work from top to the bottom in continuous brush strokes. To keep the brush rigid, hold the bristles against the surface with the handle tilted slightly toward you. Repeat until the desired effect is achieved.

3 Wipe the paintbrush occasionally on a clean, dry rag to remove excess glaze and ensure a uniform strié look. Or, rinse the brush in clear water, and wipe it dry.

4 For softer lines, brush the surface lightly after the glaze has dried for about 5 minutes. Use a soft natural-bristle brush, keeping the brush stokes in the same direction as the streaks.

Techniques for Applying a Combed Finish

Tools for combing include the Wagner Stipple and Drag pad (with edging tool), metal and rubber combs, and a notched rubber squeegee. You can make your own combing tools by notching an artist's eraser or cutting V grooves into a piece of mat board.

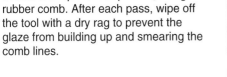

Create a unique check pattern, using a rubber comb. After each pass, wipe off the tool with a dry rag to prevent the glaze from building up and smearing the comb lines.

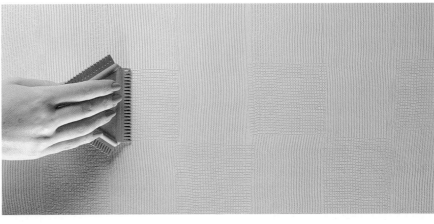

A Wagner Stipple and Drag pad can make a variety of combing designs. For a denim look, drag the pad through the glaze vertically, then horizontally

Use a rubber squeegee for swirls, scallops, and wavy lines. Wipe off excess glaze frequently to ensure clean lines.

Faux Moiré Finish

*T*he watermarked look of silk moiré fabric can be created using a rocker tool designed for wood graining (page 160). A paint glaze is applied over a base coat of paint, and the graining tool is pulled and rocked through the glaze to create impressions. Then, a dry paintbrush is pulled across the markings to mimic the crosswise grain of moiré. This dramatic tone-on-tone finish is recommended for small areas, such as the space below a chair rail or within frame moldings.

The bright sheen that is characteristic of moiré fabric is simulated by using a darker shade of low-luster latex enamel for the base coat and a lighter shade for the top coat glaze. You can use the same paint for both coats by lightening the top coat with white paint.

The glaze used for faux moiré contains more paint than most glazes, making it thicker and more opaque. Apply the glaze to a small area at a time so that you will have enough time to finish the graining before the glaze dries. If you are finishing the wall area below a chair rail or border, work from the chair rail down to the baseboard in 12"-wide sections.

How to Apply a Faux Moiré Finish

TOOLS & MATERIALS

- Wood-graining rocker tool
- Paint roller or paintbrush, for applying base coat and glaze
- Natural-bristle paintbrush, 2" to 3" wide, for dry brushing
- Low-luster latex enamel paint in darker shade, for base coat

- Low-luster enamel paint in lighter shade, or white paint to lighten base color, for glaze
- Latex paint conditioner
- Rags

FAUX MOIRÉ GLAZE

Mix together the following ingredients:
    2 parts semigloss latex enamel paint
    1 part latex paint conditioner
    1 part water

1 Apply the base coat of low-luster latex enamel, using a paint roller or paintbrush. Allow the paint to dry.

2 Mix the glaze for the top coat. Apply an even coat of glaze over the base, rolling or brushing vertically. Work in small areas to ensure the paint remains wet as you work it.

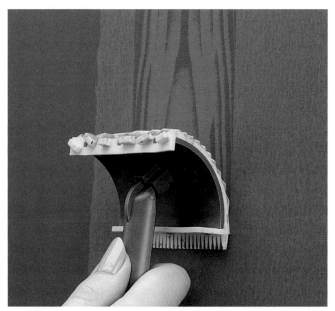

3 Slide the graining tool vertically through the wet glaze, occasionally rocking it slowly back and forth, to create the water-marked effect. Start at one corner, working in one continuous motion as you slide and rock the tool from one end to another. The simultaneous rocking and sliding motions create elongated oval markings.

4 Repeat step 3 for subsequent rows. Stagger the oval markings so that they appear randomly placed, and work quickly before glaze dries. Wipe the excess glaze from the tool as necessary, using a dry rag.

5 When the glaze has partially dried, pull a dry natural-bristle paintbrush horizontally across the surface; this mimics the crosswise grain of the moiré fabric. Wipe excess glaze from the brush as necessary. Allow the paint to dry.

Texturized Designs

Numerous household items and painting supplies can be used with paint glaze to achieve finishes that have visual texture. Rolled or bent pieces of corrugated cardboard, cheesecloth, crumpled paper, raffia, plastic wrap, fabric, and twine create interesting textured effects. The list of items is as endless as your imagination.

For these finishes, use the texturizing glaze and instructions on page 226. After applying a coat of glaze directly to the surface in a 4' × 4' section, you can either manipulate it or partially remove it by dabbing the glaze with the item or items you have selected. Or, using an alternate method, the glaze may be applied to the selected items, then printed onto the surface in small sections at a time. To become familiar with the methods and determine which effects you prefer, experiment with both techniques, using a variety of items.

Apply a base coat of paint, using a good-quality, low-luster latex enamel, before you apply the glaze. The base coat and the glaze may be in contrasting colors, such as emerald green over white. For a more subtle look, try a tone-on-tone effect, such as two shades of blue, or choose colors that are similar in intensity, such as deep red over deep purple. For even more possibilities, the process can be repeated, using one or more additional colors of glaze. This adds even more visual interest and is especially suitable when decorating small accessories.

TOOLS & MATERIALS

- Paint roller or paintbrush
- Items for creating textural effect.
- Sponge applicator
- Low-luster latex enamel paint, for base coat
- Latex or craft acrylic paint in desired sheen, for glaze
- Latex paint conditioner

How To Texturize with Cardboard

Roll a strip of corrugated cardboard and secured it with masking tape. Use the corrugated end to make a design in a coat of wet glaze.

Or, apply the glaze directly to the cardboard, using a sponge applicator. Blot the cardboard onto a paper towel, and print the designs on the surface.

Make a printing block, using single-face corrugated cardboard and a piece of stiff foam or block of wood. Glue the cardboard to the foam or wood so the corrugated lines are facing out. Create the design by pressing the block into a coat of wet glaze.

For the opposite color effect, apply the glaze to the corrugated face of the block. Blot the block, and print the impressions onto the surface.

How to Texturize with Cheesecloth

Fold a piece of cheesecloth into a flat pad and press the pad into the coat of wet glaze. To capture the weave of the cloth, lift off the pad without wiping or smearing the surface

For a more definite weave texture, apply the glaze directly to the cheesecloth pad, using a sponge applicator. Then, imprint the cheesecloth onto the surface.

How to Texturize with Paper

Crumple a piece of paper, and press into the coat of wet glaze. Experiment with other types of paper and different crumpled textures.

Or, apply the glaze to the paper with a sponge applicator. Press the paper onto the surface, crumpling and rolling the paper for a random texture.

How to Texturize with Plastic Wrap

Wrinkle the plastic wrap slightly and place it onto the coat of wet glaze. Press the wrap lightly, then peel it off the surface.

Or, apply the glaze directly to the plastic wrap, using a sponge applicator. Place the plastic on the surface, folding and crinkling it for a varied texture, then peel it away from the surface.

How to Texturize with a Fan Brush

Use a fan brush to make uniform rows of fan-shaped impressions. Press the brush into a wet glaze, and clean or blot the bristles as necessary.

For a different effect, use a fan brush to apply the glaze to the surface. To create light, wispy impressions, keep the brush as dry as possible.

How to Texturize with Fabric

Fanfold a narrow length of burlap or other coarse fabric into a thick pad. Apply a glaze to the pad, using a sponge applicator. Press the pad onto the surface. Flip the folds to the back of the pad as they become saturated, exposing fresh fabric for texturizing.

Create a different pattern by crumpling a piece of coarse fabric into loose, irregular folds. Apply the glaze with a sponge applicator, and press the fabric onto the surface. Recrumple or start with a fresh piece as the fabric becomes saturated.

How to Texturize with Twine or String

To texturize with a distinctive pattern, use the twine or string as it comes in a spool or ball. Apply a glaze, using a sponge applicator, then roll the spool or ball over the surface. Unwind the twine or string as it becomes saturated to expose fresh material for texturing.

For a more irregularly shaped pattern, wind string or twine into a tangle or a misshapen ball. Apply a glaze, then press or roll the pattern onto the surface.

Rag-rolled Designs

Rag rolling is a painting technique that gives a rich, textural look with an all-over mottled effect. It works well for walls and other flat surfaces, such as dresser tops and drawers, shelves, bookends, and doors. The rag-rolling glaze on page 232 can be used in either of the two techniques for rag rolling: *ragging-on* and *ragging-off.*

In ragging-on, a rag is saturated in the prepared paint glaze, wrung out, rolled up, then rolled across a surface that has been base-coated with low-luster latex enamel paint. For a bold pattern, rag-on a single application of glaze over the base coat. Or, for a more subtle, blended look, rag-on two or more applications of glaze.

In ragging-off, a coat of paint glaze is applied over the base coat with a paintbrush or paint roller. A rolled-up rag is then rolled over the surface to remove some of the wet glaze, revealing the base coat. This process may be repeated for more blending, but the work must be done quickly, before the glaze dries.

If you are using the ragging-off method on large surfaces, such as walls, it is helpful to have an assistant. After one person applies the glaze, the second person can rag-off the area before the glaze dries. While it is not necessary to complete the entire room in one session, it is important that you complete an entire wall.

With either method, test the technique and the colors that you intend to use on a large piece of cardboard, such as mat board, before you start the project. Generally, a lighter color is used for the base coat, with a darker color for the glaze.

Feel free to experiment with the technique as you test it, perhaps rag rolling two different glaze colors over the base coat. Or, try taping off an area, such as a border strip, and rag rolling a second or third color within the taped area.

Because the glaze can be messy to work with, apply a wide painter's tape around the area to be painted and use drop cloths to protect the surrounding surfaces. Wear old clothes and rubber gloves, and keep an old towel nearby to wipe your hands after you wring out the rags.

How to Apply a Rag-rolled Finish Using the Ragging-on Method

TOOLS & MATERIALS

- Paintbrush or paint roller
- Paint pail
- Paint tray
- Painter's masking tape
- Low-luster latex enamel paint, for base coat
- Latex or craft acrylic paint, for glaze
- Latex paint conditioner
- Rubber gloves
- Lint-free rags, about 24" × 24"
- Towel

RAG-ROLLING GLAZE

Mix together the following ingredients:
1 part latex or craft acrylic paint
1 part latex paint conditioner
1 part water

1 Apply a base coat of low-luster latex enamel, using a paintbrush or paint roller. Allow the paint to dry. Mix the glaze in a pail. Dip a lint-free rag into the glaze, saturating the entire rag, then wring it out well. Wipe excess glaze from your hands with an old towel.

2 Roll up the rag irregularly, then fold it to a length equal to the width of both hands.

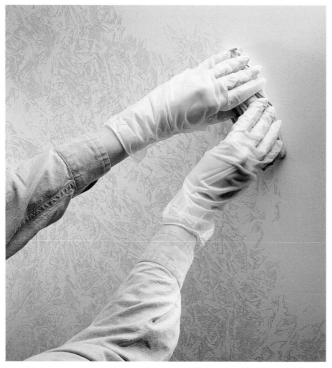

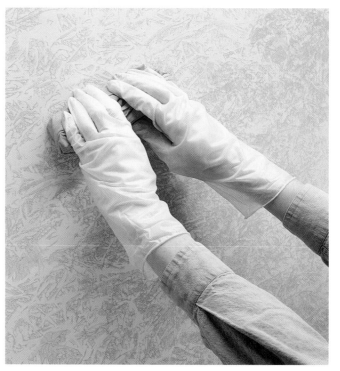

3 Roll the rag over the surface, working upward at varying angles. Rewet the rag whenever necessary, and wring it out.

4 Repeat the application, if more coverage is desired.

How to Apply a Rag-rolled Finish Using the Ragging-off Method

1 Apply base coat of low-luster latex enamel, using a paint-brush or paint roller. Allow the paint to dry. Mix the glaze (page opposite), and pour it into a paint tray. Apply the glaze over the base coat, using paint roller or paint pad.

2 Roll up a lint-free rag irregularly, then fold it to a length equal to the width of both hands. Roll the rag through the wet glaze, working upward at varying angles.

Rag-roll Variations

As shown in the examples below, the color of the base coat is not affected when the ragging-on method is used. With the ragging-off method, the color of the base coat is changed, because the glaze is applied over the entire surface.

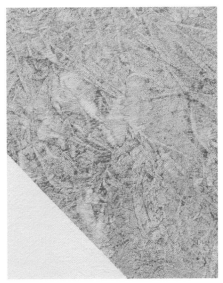

Here, the ragging-on method was used to apply an aqua glaze over a white base coat. The white base coat remained un-changed.

The ragging-off method was used here to remove some of the aqua glaze from a white base coat. Because the base was covered with the glaze, the lighter areas appear as light aqua, rather than white.

Both ragging-on and ragging-off methods were used here. First, a taupe glaze was ragged-on over a white base coat, then a rust glaze was ragged-off, changing the white base coat to a lighter shade of rust.

Blended Two Tone Finish

One of the easiest ways to give bland rooms a makeover is to paint the walls with a two-toned blended finish. Using a dual paint roller with sculptured roller covers, you can apply two different shades of paint at once to give your walls a patterned, faux-finish look. With closely related tone-on-tone paint combinations, you can create a subtle, color-washed design. For a bolder pattern, apply related shades that are next to each other on the color wheel, such as orange and yellow.

Sculptured roller covers and dual-rollers can be purchased at paint and wallcovering supply stores or home centers. For this project we chose the Wall Magic kit by Wagner, which includes a dual-roller, split paint tray, two sculptured roller covers, and sculptured finishing tools for painting in corners and around trim work.

Consider the colors in your furnishings and floor covering when choosing the paint colors. Select a combination that will harmonize with the room's existing color scheme. The easiest way to select colors is by using a monochromatic paint strip from a paint retailer. Find a strip that harmonizes with your color scheme and select paint colors that are at least two shades apart on the paint strip. For a subtle design, choose shades that are closer together; for a more patterned design, select shades that are farther apart. Or, choose a single color and a neutral shade, such as ivory or white, to create a soft, muted design.

For an added design element, use a Wagner accent roller to create a border or linear pattern over your two-tone finish. Choose a sculptured roller cover with a pleasing design and a paint color with a darker tone than the background finish.

TOOLS & MATERIALS

- Dual roller tray
- Paint stirrer stick
- Dual paint roller
- Sculptured roller covers
- Sculptured finishing tools
- Two shades of latex paint
- Paint glaze

How to Apply a Blended Two Tone Finish with a Textured Dual Roller

2 Coat the roller covers with paint and roll off any excess along the textured ramp of the tray. Apply the paint to a 4' × 4' section of wall, using arching strokes that extend up and outward in alternating directions. Turn the roller over frequently to blend the two colors. The more you roll, the more the colors will blend.

1 Pour the paints into the two sections of the paint tray. If you would like one color to dominate in your design, pour more of this color into the tray. Add ¼ cup of paint glaze to each color and blend it into the paints, using a paint stirrer stick.

Two Tone Variations

This tone-on-tone finish was created with complementary colors for a solid, blended look.

Here, a light buff color contrasts with the darker green for a deep, textured finish.

3 After rolling the 4' × 4' section, use the finishing tool to complete the design at the edges and in areas the roller couldn't reach. Dip the tool into one shade of paint and scrape off excess paint against the edge of the tray. Apply the paint to the blank areas, using a light stamping motion. Repeat with the second paint color, blending the colors to match the rolled finish.

How to Create a Border or Pattern with a Sculptured Accent Roller

Use a sculptured accent roller to create a border or pattern over your two-tone blended finish. Unlike ordinary paint rollers, you can make only a single pass in one direction with an accent roller. One application of paint to the accent roller will cover approximately 6' in a single pass. If you're painting a border, use a pencil and a carpenter's level to draw a light horizontal line along the wall. Then, mark the guideline at 6' intervals, so you'll know when to stop and reload the roller.

It's important not to saturate the entire roller when painting a border or linear pattern. Be careful to cover only the raised design on the roller cover. Fill the tray with ¼" of paint at a time, and blot excess paint with a small paintbrush or cloth. Add paint to bare areas as needed before you begin painting.

Pattern Variations

The contrasting color of this maple leaf design creates a definite border over a subtle two tone finish.

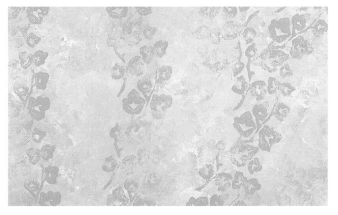

This grapevine motif appears interwoven with the two tone finish, as the accent color fades in and out.

Color Wash Finishes

Color washing is an easy paint finish that gives walls a translucent, watercolored look. It can add visual texture to flat wallboard surfaces and can emphasize the textured surfaces of plaster or stucco walls. There are two methods of color washing, each with its own glaze mixture and finished appearance.

The sponge method of color washing calls for a highly diluted glaze that is applied over a base coat of low-luster latex enamel, using a natural sea sponge. The result is a subtle texture with a soft blending of colors. The other method is color washing with a paintbrush, using a heavier glaze that holds more color than the sponge glaze. This finish retains the fine lines of the brush strokes to create a more dramatic play of tones. As the glaze begins to dry, it can be softened further by brushing the surface with a dry, natural-bristle paintbrush.

The color wash glaze can be either lighter or darker than the base coat. For best results, use two colors that are closely related, or consider using a neutral color, like beige or white, for either the base coat or the glaze. Because the glaze is messy to work with, cover the floor and furniture with drop cloths, and apply painter's tape along the ceiling and moldings.

TOOLS & MATERIALS

- Paint roller
- Flat latex paint, for glaze
- Latex paint conditioner, for sponge glaze
- Pail
- Natural sea sponge or two 3" to 4" natural-bristle paintbrushes
- Rubber gloves
- Painter's masking tape
- Waterproof drop cloths
- Low-luster latex enamel paint, for base coat

How to Color Wash with a Sponge

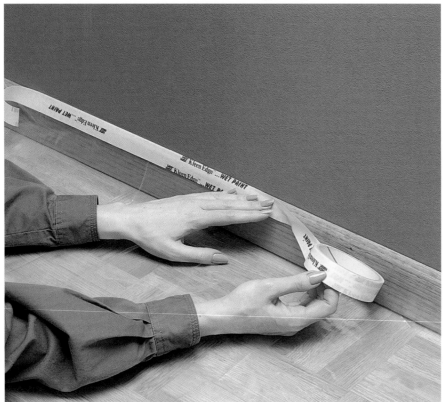

1 Mask off the surrounding area, using painter's masking tape, and cover the floor with waterproof drop cloths. Apply a base coat of low-luster latex enamel paint, using a paint roller. Allow the paint to dry.

2 Immerse the sponge into the color-washing solution. Squeeze out excess liquid, but leave the sponge very wet.

3 Beginning in a low corner, wipe the color wash solution onto the wall in short, curving strokes. Overlap and change the direction of the strokes, quickly covering a 3' × 3' section of wall.

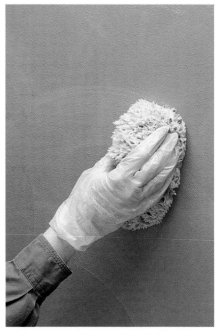

4 Repeat steps 2 and 3, moving upward and outward until the entire wall has been color washed. Allow the paint to dry. Apply a second coat, if additional color is desired.

How to Color Wash with a Brush

1 Apply a base coat of low-luster latex enamel, using a paint roller. Allow the paint to dry. Mix the color-washing glaze in a pail. Dip a paintbrush into the glaze, and remove excess glaze by scraping the brush against the rim of the pail. Apply the glaze to the wall in cross-hatching manner, beginning in one corner. The more you brush, the softer the appearance will be.

2 Brush over the surface, if desired, using a dry natural-bristle paintbrush, to soften the look. Wipe excess glaze from the brush as necessary.

Color Wash Variations

Select colors for the base coat and the glaze that are closely related, or use at least one neutral color. A darker glaze over a lighter base coat gives a mottled effect. A lighter glaze over a darker base coat gives a chalky or watercolored effect.

Here, a medium turquoise top coat was applied over a lighter base coat of white.

This finish was created with a coral base coat covered with a white top coat.

Faux Serpentine Finish

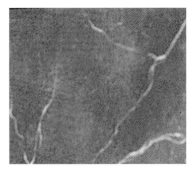

Serpentine is the general name given to a variety of green marbles that contain deposits of the mineral serpentine. The different types vary in visual texture and color tone, often with traces of black and white. Some serpentines may be characterized by a network of fine veining, while others contain little or no veining. As with other marbles, the serpentines have been used for various architectural applications, including floors, walls, and pillars.

Because genuine marble is often cut into workable pieces for installation, a faux serpentine finish applied to a large surface is more realistic if it is applied in sections with narrow grout lines (pages 250–251). By masking off alternate sections, the finish can be applied to half the project, following steps 1 to 8. When the first sections have been allowed to dry completely, they can be masked off, and the finish can be applied to the remaining sections. A high-gloss finish is then applied to the entire surface, giving the faux finish the lustrous appearance of genuine marble.

TOOLS & MATERIALS

- Low-napped paint roller, for base coat on a large surface
- Sponge applicator or paintbrush
- Stippler
- Spray bottle
- Turkey feather, for veining
- Medium green low-luster latex enamel paint, for base coat
- Craft acrylic paints in green (darker than base coat), black, and white
- Water-based clear urethane
- Newspaper
- Cheesecloth
- High-gloss clear finish or high-gloss aerosol clear acrylic sealer

How to Apply a Faux Serpentine Finish

FAUX SERPENTINE GLOSS GLAZE

Mix together the following ingredients for each gloss glaze:

1 part clear urethane
1 part paint, in desired shade
1 part water

1 Apply a base coat of medium green low-luster latex enamel to the surface, using an applicator suitable to the surface size. Apply black, green, and white gloss glazes separately in random, broad, diagonal strokes, using a sponge applicator or paintbrush. Cover most of surface, allowing small patches of the base coat to show through.

2 Stipple the glazes in adjoining areas to blend them slightly, pouncing a stippler rapidly over the surface.

3 Fold a sheet of newspaper to several layers and lay it flat over an area of the surface, in the same diagonal direction as the original paint strokes. Press the newspaper into the glaze, then lift it off, removing some of glaze.

4 Repeat step 3 over the entire surface, using the same newspaper. Occasionally turn the paper in opposite directions. Add glazes as desired to develop the color, and soften areas of high contrast by dabbing with wadded cheesecloth. Mist the surface with water, if necessary, to keep the glazes workable.

5 Brush black glaze onto a piece of newspaper and touch it to the surface diagonally in scattered areas, adding drama and depth. Soften with cheesecloth, if necessary. Repeat the process using a white glaze in small, light areas.

6 Dilute a mixture of white and green glazes with water to the consistency of light cream. Run the edge and tip of the feather through the diluted glaze. Place the tip of the feather onto the surface in the desired placement for a vein. Lightly drag the feather diagonally over the surface, fidgeting and turning it slightly, and varying the pressure, to create an irregular, jagged vein. Begin and end veins off the edge of the surface.

7 Repeat step 6 as desired to build a veining pattern. Connect adjacent vein lines occasionally to create narrow, oblong, irregular shapes. Dab veins lightly with wadded cheesecloth to soften, if necessary. Allow the surface to dry.

8 Dilute the glazes to the consistency of ink, and apply each randomly to the surface. Dab with wadded cheesecloth to soften the colors. Allow the glazes to dry. Apply several thin coats of high-gloss clear finish or high-gloss aerosol clear acrylic sealer, allowing the surface to dry between coats.

Painting Advanced Designs & Finishes   245

Faux Stone Floor Tile Designs

A painted finish that mimics unpolished stone can be applied to a floor using a stippler or pieces of newspaper. The stippling technique results in a relatively smooth textured finish with blended colors, while the newspaper method creates an unpolished stone finish with depth, color variation, and a rough visual texture. Adding rustic grout lines to either finish creates the look of expensive stone tiles.

A variety of earth-tone glazes can be combined to make a stone finish in the desired color. In general, you will need only two or three colors, because they will blend together and develop a range of tones as the finish is applied.

To create grout lines, apply masking tape to the surface in a grid pattern before applying the faux finish. You can get a rustic look by painting the lines in by hand or create the illusion of depth by "shadowing" the grout lines for a trompe l'oeil effect.

TOOLS & MATERIALS

- Low-napped roller, for base coat on a large surface
- Sponge applicator or paintbrush
- Stippler or newspaper
- Pencil
- Straightedge
- White low-luster latex enamel paint, for base coat
- Flat latex paint in two or three earth-tone shades, for flat glazes
- Latex paint conditioner
- Cheesecloth
- Flat latex paint in white and an earth-tone shade, for washes
- Matte clear finish or aerosol matte clear acrylic sealer (optional)
- ¼" masking tape, latex or craft acrylic paint in shade to contrast with stone finish, and round artist's brush, for rustic grout lines
- ⅛" masking tape, mat knife, marker, and burnishing tool, for trompe l'oeil grout lines

How to Apply a Faux Stone Finish Using the Stippling Method

1 Apply a base coat of white low-luster latex enamel to the surface, using an applicator suitable to the surface size. Allow the paint to dry. Mask off grout lines, if desired (pages 250–251).

2 Apply a flat earth-tone glaze in random strokes, using a sponge applicator or paintbrush. Cover about half of the surface. Repeat with another color glaze in the remaining areas, leaving some small areas of the base coat unglazed.

3 Stipple over the surface, using a stippler. Blend the colors as desired, leaving some areas very dark and others light enough for the base coat to show through. Add white and black glazes, or earth-tone glazes, as desired. Stipple to blend the colors and allow the paint to dry.

FAUX STONE FLAT GLAZES

Mix together the following ingredients for each shade of earth-toned flat glaze:

    1 part flat latex paint
    1 part latex paint conditioner
    1 part water

FAUX STONE WASHES

Mix together the following ingredients for each shade of wash:

    1 part flat latex paint
    2–3 parts water

Dilute paint with water until it reaches the consistency of ink.

4 Apply a white wash to the entire surface. Dab with wadded cheesecloth to soften the finish. Allow the paint to dry, then apply matte clear finish or matte aerosol clear acrylic sealer, if desired.

How to Apply a Faux Stone Finish Using the Newspaper Method

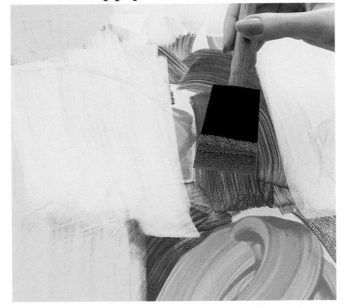

1 Follow steps 1 and 2 on page 248. Apply a white wash in desired areas, and apply an earth-tone wash in other areas.

2 Fold a sheet of newspaper to several layers. Lay it flat over one area of the surface and press it into the glaze. Lift the paper, removing some of the glaze. Repeat in other areas, using the same newspaper, turning it in different directions to blend the colors roughly.

3 Add more color to an area by spreading glaze onto the newspaper and laying it flat on the surface. Repeat as necessary until the desired effect is achieved. Leave some dark accent areas in the finish, as well as an occasional light spot. Use the same newspaper throughout. Allow the paint to dry.

4 Apply a white wash to the entire surface. Dab with a wadded cheesecloth to soften the colors. Allow the paint to dry, then apply a matte clear finish or matte aerosol clear acrylic sealer, if desired.

How to Apply Rustic Grout Lines

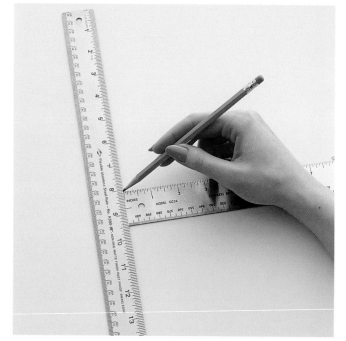

1 Apply a base coat of white low-luster latex enamel to the surface, using an applicator suitable to the surface size. Allow the paint to dry. Plan the placement of the grout lines, and mark the points of intersection, using a pencil and a straightedge.

2 Stretch ¼" masking tape taut, and apply it to the surface in horizontal lines, positioning the tape lines just under the marked points. Repeat for the vertical lines, positioning the tape just right of the marks. Press the tape firmly in place with the pads of your fingers, but do not burnish the tape.

3 Apply the desired faux finish (pages 248–249). Allow the finish to dry. Carefully remove the tape lines.

4 Paint over the grout lines freehand, using a round artist's brush and a grout line glaze in a color that contrasts pleasingly with the faux finish. Allow the lines to have some irregularity in thickness and density. Allow the paint to dry. Apply a finish or sealer to the entire surface, as desired.

How to Apply Trompe l'Oeil Grout Lines

1 Follow step 1 on page 250. Stretch ⅛" masking tape taut, and apply it to the surface in horizontal lines, positioning the tape lines just under the marked points. Repeat for the vertical lines, positioning the tape just right of the marks.

2 Cut a triangle from the horizontal tape lines, starting to the left of each intersection with the vertical tape lines, using a mat knife. Cut from the upper point of the intersection down to the lower left at a 45° angle.

GROUT LINE GLAZE

Mix together the following ingredients:
- 1 part latex or craft acrylic paint
- 1 part latex paint conditioner
- 1 part water

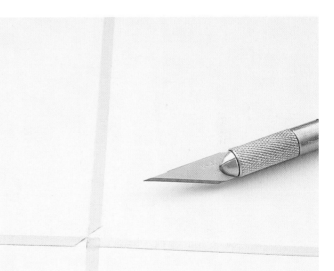

3 Cut a triangle from the vertical tape lines, just above each intersection with the horizontal tape lines. Cut from the left point of the intersection to the upper right at a 45° degree angle.

(Continued next page)

4 Burnish all of the tape lines to seal the edges, using a plastic credit card or tongue depressor. Apply the desired faux finish (pages 248–249). Allow the finish to dry thoroughly.

5 Draw in a shadow, ⅛" wide, above each horizontal tape, using a marker in a shade darker than the base-coat color. Use a straightedge for accuracy.

6 Draw in a shadow, ⅛" wide, to the left of each vertical tape. Then, carefully remove all tape from the surface. Apply a finish or sealer to the entire surface, as desired.

Grout Line Variations

Create a square tile effect by applying tape lines at evenly spaced intervals, both horizontally and vertically.

Tape a grid for a square tile effect, then remove alternate vertical sections to mimic the look of staggered stone block.

Combine grout line patterns to add interest to the faux finish.

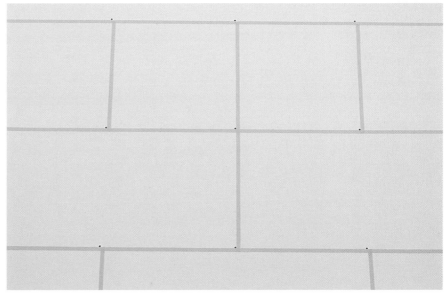

Faux Wood Grain
Floor Finish

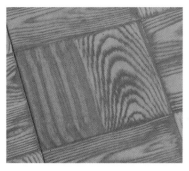

*T*he rich patterns and colors of natural wood grain can be imitated, using a technique that dates back as far as Roman times and was especially popular in the late nineteenth century. Long revered as a technique used exclusively by skilled artisans, wood graining has made a recent comeback, as new tools such as the wood-graining rocker (page 256) have become available. Wood graining is a suitable finish for any smooth surface.

For faux wood grain, a glaze of thickened paint is applied over a base coat of low-luster latex enamel. The rocker side of a wood-graining tool is dragged through the wet glaze as the tool is rocked back and forth. The simultaneuos dragging and rocking of the tool creates oval-shaped markings that simulate the characteristic grain of pine and other woods.

Become familiar with the graining technique by practicing it on a large sheet of cardboard until you can achieve a realistic look. This will also allow you to test the finish before applying it to the actual project.

To create the effect of wood parquet, mark the base coat in a grid made of 4" or 8" squares. You can center the design, or begin at one corner with a full square. Mask off alternate squares in the gridwork, and wood-grain the surface in alternating horizontal and vertical directions.

WOOD GRAINING ROCKER

Comb edge

Rocker

Notched edge

TOOLS & MATERIALS

- Synthetic-bristle paintbrush, sponge applicator, or paint roller, for applying base coat
- Synthetic-bristle paintbrush, optional for applying glaze
- Wood-graining rocker
- Soft natural-bristle paintbrush, 3" or 4" wide, for blending wood grain
- Pencil, straightedge, painter's masking tape, and putty knife, for faux wood parquet finish
- Low-luster latex enamel paint, for base coat
- Craft acrylic paint or latex paint in desired sheen, for glaze
- Acrylic paint thickener
- Rags
- Cardboard, for practicing design
- Satin or high-gloss clear finish or aerosol clear acrylic sealer

How to Paint a Faux Wood Grain Finish

The final color of the wood grain finish depends on the combined effect of the base coat and the glaze coat. For an appearance of natural wood, use a lighter base coat and overlay it with a darker glaze. Suitable colors for the base coat include raw sienna, red oxide, burnt sienna, burnt umber, and beige tones. For the glaze, good colors include burnt umber, black, red oxide, and burnt sienna. Because of the wide range of wood stains commonly used on woodwork, it is not necessary to duplicate both the grain and the color of any particular wood.

WOOD GRAINING GLAZE

Mix together the following ingredients:
2 parts craft acrylic paint or latex paint in desired sheen.
1 part acrylic paint thickener.

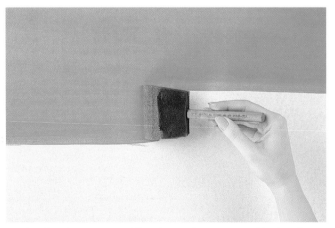

1 Apply a base coat of low-luster latex enamel in the desired color, stroking in the desired direction for the wood grain. Use a paintbrush or sponge applicator, or use a paint roller for large areas. Allow the paint to dry.

2 Mix the wood-graining glaze. Apply an even coat of glaze over the base coat to a small area at a time, using a sponge applicator or a synthetic-bristle paintbrush. Stroke the brush in the desired direction for the wood grain.

3 Slide the wood-graining rocker through the wet glaze, rocking it slowly to create the wood-grain effect. Start at one corner, working in one continuous motion as you slide and rock the tool from one end to another (above). The position of the rocker corresponds to the wood grain markings, as shown here.

4 Repeat step 3 for subsequent rows, varying the space between the oval markings. Wipe excess glaze from the tool as necessary, using a dry rag. For some rows, pull the comb or notched edge of the wood-graining tool through the glaze, instead of using the rocker portion. This varies the look by giving it a simple, continuous wood grain.

5 Brush across the surface before the glaze is completely dry, using a dry, soft natural-bristle paintbrush, (3" to 4" wide). Lightly brush in the direction of the wood grain to soften the finish. Wipe excess glaze from the brush, as necessary. Allow the glaze to dry. Apply a clear finish or aerosol clear acrylic sealer, if desired.

How to Paint a Faux Wood Parquet Finish

1 Apply a base coat of low-luster latex enamel, using a paint-brush or paint roller. Allow the paint to dry. Measure and mark a grid over the base coat, using a straightedge and pencil. Center the grid or begin with a complete square at one corner.

2 Apply painter's masking tape to alternate squares in the grid. Use a putty knife to trim the masking tape diagonally at the corners, as shown. Press firmly along the edges of tape, to prevent the glaze from seeping through. Mix the wood-graining glaze (page 256).

3 Apply the glaze to the unmasked squares, brushing in a horizontal di-rection. Slide the wood-graining rocker horizontally through the wet glaze on some squares, for a straight wood-grain effect. Rock the tool horizontally on the remaining squares, varying the positions of the oval markings. Work on only a few squares at a time, because the glaze dries quickly.

4 Brush across the surface before the glaze is completely dry, using a dry, soft, natural-bristle paintbrush. Brush lightly in the direction of the wood grain, to soften the finish. Wipe excess glaze from the brush as necessary, using a dry rag.

5 Allow the paint to dry, then remove the masking tape. Apply new masking tape over the wood-grained squares. Apply glaze to the unmasked squares, brushing in a vertical direction. Repeat steps 3 and 4, working in a vertical direc-tion. Allow the paint to dry, then remove the masking tape. Apply a clear finish or aerosol clear acrylic sealer, if desired.

Wood Grain Variations

You can create wood tones that resemble common wood stains, such as cherry, honey oak, and walnut, by choosing specific paint colors for the base coat and glaze.

A cherry finish is duplicated by using a dark rust base coat and a burnt umber glaze.

Honey oak is mimicked by using a light tan base coat and a golden tan glaze.

Walnut stain is created by using a dark gold base coat and a burnt umber glaze.

Decorating with Advanced Techniques

J ust as modern paints and glazes make it possible for do-it-yourselfers to acheive wonderful custom paint finishes, there is a wide range of new wallcovering and molding products now available that let you add exciting architectural dimensions to your decorating scheme. In this final section of the book, we'll show you five techniques for giving your home a truly hand-crafted look.

Specialty wallcoverings, such as fabrics and embossed materials, can be fragile and difficult to work with, as well as expensive, but their natural or textured surfaces add more than just color to a wall. On the following pages, we'll give you some essential tips for preparing your walls and show you how to handle and install specialty materials for flawless results.

Decorating with wallcovering cutouts is a surprisingly easy project that can have a dramatic impact on a room. By cutting out motifs from strips of standard wallcovering and pasting them on a wall, you can highlight a picture or a particular furnishing. When set into the solid background of a painted wall, cutouts can simulate the look of three-dimensional objects, creating a delightful trompe l'oeil effect.

Building a cornice for a window may seem difficult, but you can do it easily by combining basic wallcovering techniques with simple plywood box construction. The cornice project in this section shows how to measure and build the plywood frame to fit around existing window treatments and cover it with a wallcovering border of your choosing.

Decorative moldings add a permanent elegance to an interior space, and do-it-youselfers now have many options to choose from. For example, you can create wall frame moldings using basic wood trim available at any home center. Or, you can choose from among the many new polyurethane products now available from specialty retailers and catalog vendors. Whichever products you choose, this section will show you the tools and basic installation techniques you'll need do the job.

Specialty Wallcoverings

Specialty wallcoverings can add new interest to a room. The basic hanging methods are the same as for standard wall-coverings (pages 116–155), but specialty wallcoverings do require some special handling techniques. Reflective wallcoverings, such as foils and mylars, can add light to even the darkest rooms, but the walls must be perfectly smooth before hanging. Fabric or grasscloth wallcoverings can soften and hide flaws in irregular walls, but they are difficult to keep clean. Embossed wallcoverings also hide flawed walls, but do not soil as easily as fabrics and grasscloths.

For very rough walls, consider hanging a liner paper before the wallcovering. Liner paper strips are hung horizontally so that the wallcovering seams cannot overlap the liner seams.

Always follow the manufacturer's directions when hanging specialty wallcoverings, and make your selection carefully: Specialty wallcoverings can be expensive.

Tips for Working with Fabric Wallcoverings

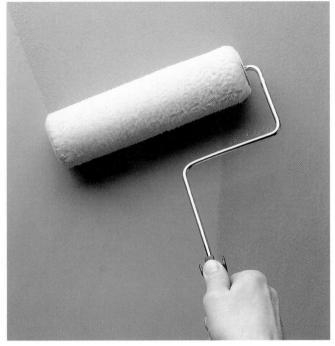 

Use a clear adhesive or traditional wheat paste, as directed by the manufacturer. Clear adhesive will not bleed through and stain fabric surfaces. Some wallcoverings may direct you to apply adhesive to the walls rather than to the strips.

Use a dry paint roller with a soft nap, or a soft brush with natural bristles to smooth flocks and fabrics. A brush with stiff bristles might damage the wallcovering surface.

Tips for Working with Foil Wallcoverings

Apply liner paper to create a smooth base for wallcovering over rough or uneven surfaces, such as paneled, textured or masonry walls.

Handle foils carefully. Do not crease or wrinkle the strips, and make sure to flatten out all bubbles immediately when hanging.

Use a soft smoothing brush to avoid scratching or burnishing the reflective surface. Do not roll the seams: tap gently with a smoothing brush to bond seams.

Tips for Working with Embossed Wallcoverings

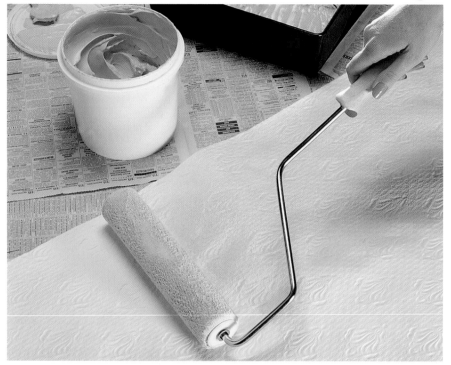

Apply a clay-based wallcovering adhesive to the back side of the wallcovering strips, using a paint roller. Take care not to press the roller too hard against the paper. Too much pressure can damage the embossed pattern.

Gently tap seams with a smoothing brush to bond them. Do not use a seam roller on embossed wallcoverings.

Keep adhesive off the face of embossed wallcoverings, if possible. Remove wet adhesive immediately by blotting gently with a slightly damp sponge.

Finish embossed wallcoverings with several coats of latex paint. Use a paintbrush, working the paint evenly into the crevices. Let the paint dry between coats.

Embossed Wallcovering Finish Variations

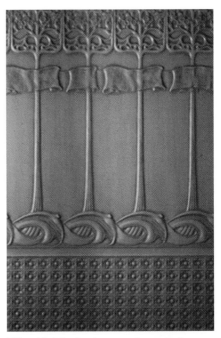

Clouding finish: Apply two coats of alkyd paint for the base tone. Combine a darker, related shade of alkyd paint with clear glaze, applying it over the first coat.

Gold highlighting: Start by priming the wallcovering with acrylic primer. Then, apply two coats of latex eggshell finish paint for the base coat. Apply a gold glaze to the raised details with a small artist's brush.

Wiped finish: Apply an undercoat of acrylic white primer, followed by two coats of white alkyd paint. Combine high gloss enamel in the desired over-tone with clear glaze, and "wipe" it onto the surface with a cotton rag.

Faux tin finish: Apply two coats of satin latex in white, one coat of latex metallic paint in silver, one coat of oak-toned glaze, and a final coat of semi-gloss varnish.

Antiqued leather finish: Apply two coats of satin latex as a base tone, followed by a coat of dark-toned glaze applied in small sections. Partially remove the glaze with a cotton rag. Finish with a final coat of semi-gloss varnish.

Wallcovering Cutouts

Wallcovering cutouts are design motifs that are cut from wallcovering strips or borders. The cutout designs can be used to create interesting patterns or trompe l'oeil effects on painted walls. Unique designs can be created by combining motifs from different wallcoverings. For best results, walls should be painted with a high-grade washable paint, such as a low-luster or satin-sheen paint, or a flat enamel.

For most wall applications, a clear vinyl adhesive will bond cutouts to the wall surface. If you are applying a border adhesive to prepasted cutouts, you may want to remove the prepasted glue to reduce the thickness of the paper. Remove the glue by soaking the cutout in water and lightly rubbing the pasted side. Blot the cutout with a towel to remove excess water, then apply the desired adhesive.

How to Apply a Wallcovering Cutout

TOOLS & MATERIALS

- Mat knife or small scissors
- Cutting surface
- Sponge applicator
- Sponge
- Seam roller
- Wallcovering or border strips
- Plastic or wax paper
- Wallcovering adhesive

1 Cut out the wallcovering motifs, using a mat knife and a cutting surface or small, sharp scissors. Simplify the designs as necessary. For easier handling, make any interior cuts before trimming the outer edges.

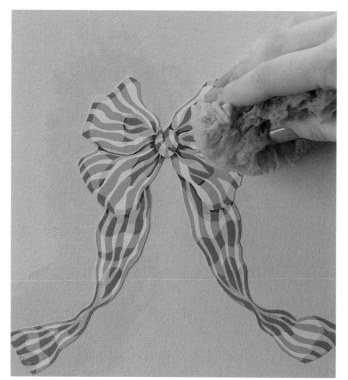

2 Place the cutout facedown on a sheet of plastic or wax paper. Gently brush on a thin, even layer of adhesive, using a sponge applicator.

3 Press the cutout onto the surface. Smooth out any air bubbles, using a damp sponge. Roll the edges firmly with a seam roller. Rinse off any excess adhesive, using a damp sponge.

Laser Cut Borders

Laser cut borders, available at paint and wallcovering stores, offer the detail of a wallcovering cutout in a continuous border strip. The outlines of the design motifs are cut with a laser for perfect accuracy. Laser cut borders may be prepasted or unpasted and can be installed using the methods for standard wallcovering borders (pages 150–151).

Tips for Decorating with Cutouts

Create a focal point with pictures or plates by using design motifs, like ribbons or ropes, as faux hangers. Mark the position of the picture or plate first, then cut the wallcovering motifs for display above and below the object.

Extend the length of a design by cutting it apart and spreading the sections. Fill in the space between sections with smaller motifs, such as flowers, rosettes, or bows.

Plan the placement by positioning cutouts temporarily with poster putty. Mark the positions lightly with a pencil, or use positioned pieces as a guide when securing each motif in place.

Wallcovering Cornices

*U*se wallcovering borders and plywood to create sleek, tailored cornices. These cornices are especially attractive when used with simple undertreatments, such as shades, blinds, and sheer curtain panels. For a finished look, paint the edges of the cornice to match or coordinate with the edge of the wallcovering border.

Determine the inside measurements for the cornice only after any undertreatment is in place. The cornice should clear the undertreatment by 2" to 3", and it should extend beyond the end brackets of the hanging rod by at least 2" on each side. Choose a wallcovering border that is wide enough for the completed cornice to cover any drapery heading and hardware.

TOOLS & MATERIALS

- Measuring tape, ruler
- Sponge applicator or paintbrush
- ½" finish plywood with smooth finish on at least one side.
- Circular saw or hand saw
- Hammer
- Nail set
- Wallcovering border
- Border adhesive
- Wood glue

- 16ga. × 1½" brads
- Wood filler, putty knife
- Medium-grit sandpaper
- Primer, suitable for paint and wallcovering
- Paint to coordinate with or match the edge of wallcovering border
- Angle irons
- Pan-head screws or molly bolts

How to Cut the Plywood & Wallcovering Border

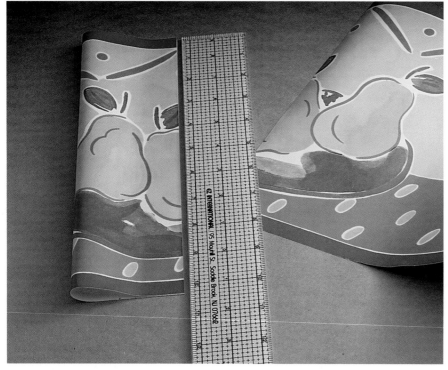

First, determine the expanded width of the wallcovering border by applying border adhesive to a 6" length of border. Fold the border in half lengthwise. Allow the adhesive to set for about 5 minutes, then remeasure the width. This is the actual height to cut the cornice front and side pieces.

Determine the inside measurements of the cornice, taking into account any clearance for window treatments and trim moldings. Cut the plywood for the top piece to match these dimensions.

Cut the front piece of the cornice to a height that equals the expanded width of the border, and a length equal to that of the top piece, plus 1".

Cut the side pieces to a height equal to that of the expanded width of the border, and a length equal to the width of the top piece.

How to Construct the Cornice

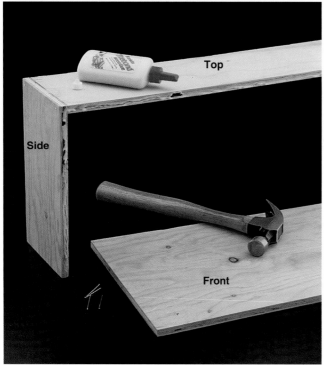

1 Attach the side pieces to the ends of the top piece, using glue and nails. Glue and nail the front piece, keeping the edges flush with the outside faces of the top and side pieces. Countersink the nails, using a nail set. Fill the nail holes with wood filler. Also fill any voids in the front, sides, and lower edges of the plywood. Sand all of the surfaces smooth.

2 Apply primer to all of the cornice surfaces and allow it to dry. Paint the lower edges and the top of the cornice, extending the paint slightly over the edges to the front and sides. Paint the entire inside surface of the cornice.

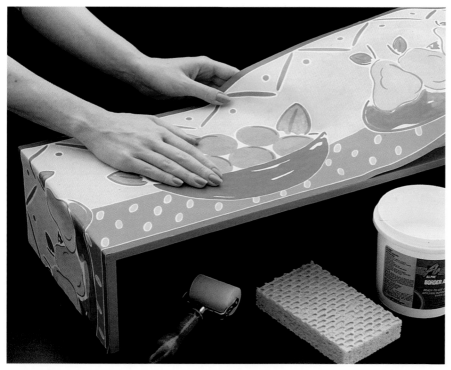

3 Cut the wallcovering border equal to the distance around the sides and front of the cornice plus 4". Prepare the border as for unpasted wallcovering (page 129), using border adhesive. Center the border on the cornice, wrapping the ends around the back edges of the cornice to just cover the inside edges of the plywood. Trim excess paper.

4 Secure angle irons on the inside of the cornice top, one at each end and every 45" along the back edge of the top piece. Hold the cornice at the desired placement, and make sure it is level. Mark the angle iron screw holes on the wall or window frame. Remove the angle irons. Secure the irons to the wall, using pan-head screws driven into wall studs (use molly bolts where the irons fall between wall studs.) Reattach the cornice to the installed angle irons.

Cornice Variations

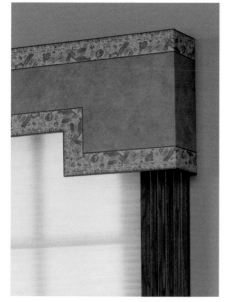

Here, a border edging strip was cut from a companion wallcovering border and used to trim the upper and lower edges of a shaped cornice.

A scalloped border defines the shape of the lower edge of this cornice. Curved lines can be cut with jig saw fitted with a fine-tooth blade.

To increase the height of the cornice, a section of the edge pattern was added beneath the wallcovering border.

Wall Frame Moldings

*A*dd architectural detail to a living room by installing molding in a picture-type frame on the walls. Frame molding can be used to accent special features of the room, divide large walls into smaller sections, and add interest to otherwise plain walls. The molding may be the same color as the walls, or a contrasting color. The effect can be intensified by painting the wall area within the frame molding a different color or by applying a wallcovering to the inset area.

Simple, decorative wood moldings, available at home centers and lumber yards in a wide variety of styles, work best for wall frames. To determine the size and location of the frames, cut strips of paper the width of the molding and experiment with different frame sizes by taping the strips to the wall. Where possible, try to size the frame molding so it matches the dimension of some architectural detail in the room—such as the width of windows or a fireplace.

Install the molding with small finish nails near the outside corners of the molding and at wall stud locations; use nails long enough to go through the wall surface and into the studs. If you aren't able to locate wall studs where you need them, apply small dots of wood glue or construction adhesive to the back of the molding to secure the frame pieces to the wall.

TOOLS & MATERIALS

- Wood molding
- Butcher paper, for strips
- Masking tape
- Carpenter's level and pencil
- Measuring tape
- Miter box and backsaw, or power miter saw
- Drill and 1/16" bit

- 6d finish nails
- Hammer
- Nail set
- Wood glue or construction adhesive, if necessary
- Paint and paintable latex caulk, or wood stain and putty to match stain
- Paintbrush

How to Install Wall Frame Moldings

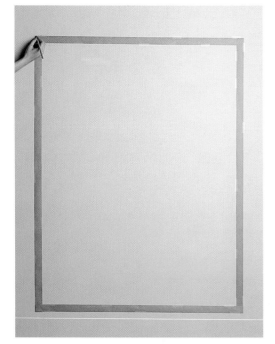

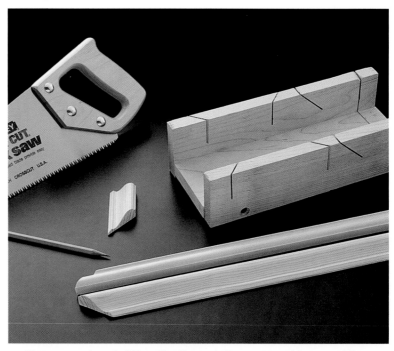

1 Cut paper strips to the width of the molding, and tape them to the wall. Mark the placement for the outer edge of the top molding piece with light pencil lines. Use a carpenter's level to make sure the marks are level.

2 Measure and mark 45° cutting lines on the upper and lower molding pieces. Cut the pieces, using a miter box and a back saw. The top and bottom pieces should be the same length. Repeat to cut the side strips. Test fit the first molding, and if satisfied, cut pieces for all other moldings to match the dimensions of the first pieces.

3 Paint or stain the moldings, as desired. Drill pilot holes with a ¹⁄₁₆" drill bit. Position the top molding piece on the wall, aligning it with the placement marks. Apply small dots of glue to the back of the molding, where necessary. Nail the moldings to the wall, leaving the nail heads slightly above the surface.

4 Attach the side molding pieces, placing a partially driven nail at the upper ends only. Fit the bottom piece, making sure the frame is square. Adjust the frame, if necessary, so that all of the joints fit tightly at the corners. Then, secure the pieces with nails and glue.

5 Drive the nails slightly below the surface, using a nail set. Fill the nail holes and corner joints with paintable latex caulk, if the molding is painted, or wood putty, if it is stained. Touch up the patched areas with paint or stain.

Wall Frame Molding Variations

These framed areas are wallcovered, creating depth and interest in an otherwise plain wall.

The double moldings on this wall emphasize the architectural detailing.

Contrasting molding calls special attention to the artwork in this traditional grouping.

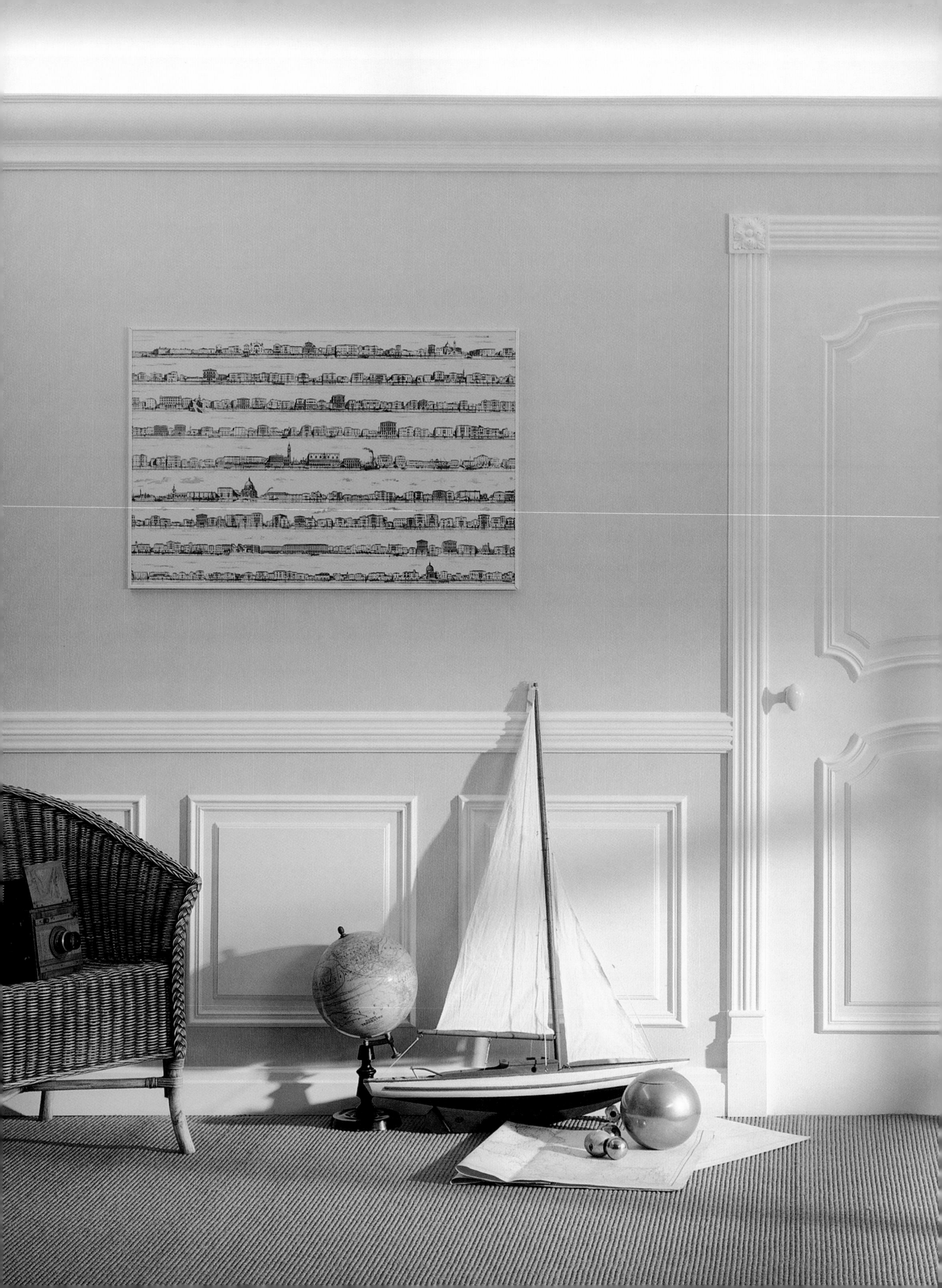

Decorative Moldings

*A*dd a dramatic accent to a room with polyurethane moldings. Polyurethane moldings have the look of cast plaster and hand-carved wood moldings but are lighter and easier to install than moldings made with traditional materials. Polyurethane products are manufactured to replicate historical styles for a variety of architectural elements, including crown and trim moldings, ceiling medallions, pilasters, corbels, and raised panels.

Polyurethane moldings can be painted the same color as the walls or ceiling, painted with a contrasting color, decorated with a faux finish design, or treated with a wood stain. Another option is to highlight the intricate raised designs by painting the raised patterns in one or more contrasting colors.

Using a special adhesive, you can attach polyurethane moldings to most interior surfaces. To ensure good adhesion and an even finish, you'll need to prepare the surface—clean the walls, remove any old wallcovering, repair loose or damaged plaster or wallboard, and prime or sand the surface (see pages 62–87). To prevent warping, store the moldings in the room where they will be installed for 24 hours prior to installation. Avoid installing the molding when the humidity level is greater than 70%.

When installing patterned moldings, begin the installation at the most visible corner so that you can easily match the pattern. Finish the installation at an inconspicuous corner, where an unmatched pattern will be less obvious.

How to Install a Ceiling Medallion Above a Chandelier

A ceiling medallion is an elegant accent that can highlight a chandelier or other light fixture and establish a visual center point in a room. Removing a chandelier is easy and safe if you make sure to turn off the power to the fixture at the main service panel and have a helper support the weight of the chandelier while you disconnect it.

To determine how your chandelier is supported, examine the decorative coverplate at the ceiling. There should be either a retaining nut in the center, or two or more nuts or screws on the surface of the coverplate. This hardware may support the weight of the fixture, so have a helper support the fixture as you remove the nuts and the coverplate.

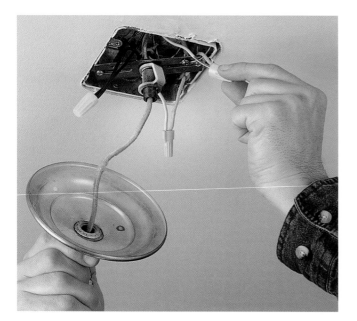

1 Turn off the power to the light fixture at the main service panel. Unscrew the coverplate retaining nut or screws and lower the coverplate to expose the wire connections. Disconnect the fixture wires from the home's circuit wires by removing the wire connectors. The fixture wire marked with lettering or a colored stripe is the neutral wire; it is connected to the white circuit wire. The unmarked fixture wire is hot and is connected to the black circuit wire.

Most chandeliers are supported by a threaded nipple that is screwed into a mounting strap attached to the electrical box. Unscrew this nipple and set the fixture out of the way. If the fixture is supported by a coverplate that is screwed or bolted directly to the mounting strap, you can remove the fixture once the wires are disconnected.

TOOLS & MATERIALS
- Screwdriver, adjustable wrench, or channel-type pliers
- Pencil
- Drill, circle cutter, piloting and countersink bits
- Caulk gun
- Cordless screwdriver
- Polyurethane ceiling medallion
- 150-grit sandpaper
- Polyurethane adhesive
- Wallboard screws
- Paintable latex caulk or filler

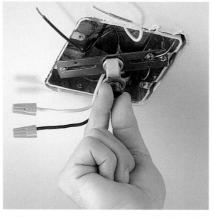

2 To compensate for the added thickness of the medallion, unscrew the threaded nipple and replace it with a longer one, or buy longer screws that will reach from the coverplate to the mounting strap.

3 Lightly sand the back of the medallion with 150-grit sandpaper. Adjust a circle cutter to cut a hole through the medallion that is smaller than the chandelier coverplate but large enough to provide access to the screw holes on the mounting strap. Cut the hole for the center of the medallion, using the circle cutter and a power drill. Position the medallion on the ceiling, centering the hole over the electrical box, and draw a light pencil line to mark its placement on the ceiling.

4 Apply polyurethane adhesive to the back of the medallion. Run the bead in a serpentine pattern and keep the adhesive 1" away from the outer edge of the medallion. Carefully align the medallion within the penciled outline and press it onto the ceiling. Drill several countersunk pilot holes through the medallion in inconspicuous areas. Then, drive wallboard screws through the pilot holes and into the ceiling to hold the medallion in place while the glue dries. Be careful not to tighten the screws too much.

5 Fill the screw holes with paintable latex caulk or filler, and wipe away any excess caulk with a damp cloth or a wet finger. Smooth the caulk over the holes so it is flush with the surface of the medallion. Paint or stain the medallion, if desired, and let the finish dry completely. Reattach the chandelier.

Molding Finish Variations

The great variety of polyurethane moldings allows you to combine styles and architectural elements for a distinctive decorative addition to any room.

Here, raised panels add depth to the flat wall and door surfaces. The door frame is trimmed with pilasters, a lintel, and corner blocks. On the wall, a sconce provides a pleasing fan of light.

This wall is topped with an elaborate cornice molding. Crown and cornice moldings can be combined with other types of trim, such as casing, base, and panel moldings, to enhance the design.

In this scheme, the intricate detail of the ceiling medallion is offset by the Victorian crown molding. A classical corbel serves as a decorative anchor for the archway.

How to Install Crown Molding

TOOLS & MATERIALS

- Caulk gun
- Cordless screwdriver
- Measuring tape, pencil
- Hammer
- Putty knife
- Drill, piloting and countersink bits
- Power miter saw or hand miter box and fine-tooth saw
- Polyurethane crown molding
- Spackling compound and putty knife
- Polyurethane adhesive
- 2" wallboard screws
- Finish nails
- Paintable latex caulk or filler

1 Plan the layout of the molding pieces by measuring the walls of the room and making light pencil marks at the joint locations. For each piece that starts or ends at a corner, add 1' to 2' to compensate for the waste resulting from miter cutting the end. Avoid pieces less than 3' long, if possible, because shorter pieces are more difficult to fit.

2 Hold a section of molding against the wall and ceiling in the finished position. Make light pencil marks on the wall every 1' along the bottom edge of the molding. Remove the molding and tack a finish nail at each pencil mark: these will hold the molding in place while the adhesive dries. If the wall is plaster, drill pilot holes for the nails.

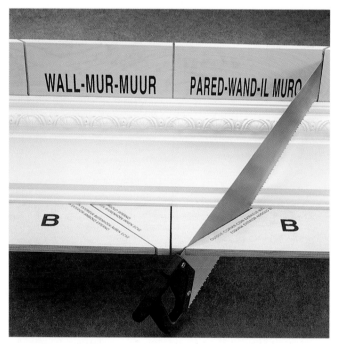

3 Start the first molding pieces at the most conspicuous corner to be sure the pattern will match. To make the miter cuts for the first corner, position the molding face up in a miter box. Set the ceiling-side edge of the molding flat against the horizontal base of the miter box, and set the wall-side edge against the vertical back fence. Make the cut at 45°.

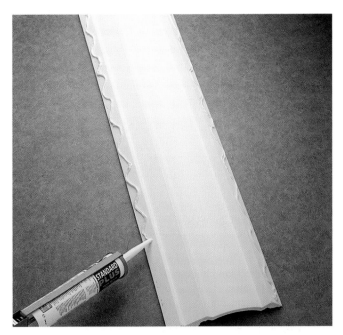

4 Check the uncut ends of each molding piece before installing it. Make sure mating pieces will butt together squarely in a tight joint. Cut all square ends at 90°, using the miter saw or hand miter box.

5 Lightly sand the back edges of the molding that will make contact with the wall and ceiling, using 150-grit sandpaper. Wipe away the sanding dust, using a rag slightly dampened with mineral spirits. Run a small bead of polyurethane adhesive along both sanded edges.

6 Set the molding in place with the mitered end tight to the corner and the bottom edge resting on the finish nails. Press along the wall and ceiling edges to create a good bond. At both ends of the molding section, drill a countersunk pilot hole through the top and bottom edges and into the ceiling and wall. Drive a wallboard screw through each pilot hole to secure the molding in place.

7 Cut, sand, and glue the next section of molding. Apply a bead of adhesive to the end of the installed molding where it will butt against the new section. Install the new section, and secure the ends with screws, making sure the joints are aligned properly. Install the remaining molding sections and allow the adhesive to dry.

8 Carefully remove the finish nails and fill the nail holes with spackling compound. Fill the screw holes in the molding and any gaps in the joints with paintable latex caulk or filler, and wipe away excess caulk with a damp cloth or a wet finger. Smooth the caulk over the holes so it is flush with the surface.

Converting Measurements

To Convert:	To:	Multiply by:
Inches	Millimeters	25.4
Inches	Centimeters	2.54
Feet	Meters	0.305
Yards	Meters	0.914
Square inches	Square centimeters	6.45
Square feet	Square meters	0.093
Square yards	Square meters	0.836
Cubic inches	Cubic centimeters	16.4
Cubic feet	Cubic meters	0.0283
Cubic yards	Cubic meters	0.765
Ounces	Milliliters	30.0
Pints (U.S.)	Liters	0.473 (Imp. 0.568)
Quarts (U.S.)	Liters	0.946 (Imp. 1.136)
Gallons (U.S.)	Liters	3.785 (Imp. 4.546)
Ounces	Grams	28.4
Pounds	Kilograms	0.454

To Convert:	To:	Multiply by:
Millimeters	Inches	0.039
Centimeters	Inches	0.394
Meters	Feet	3.28
Meters	Yards	1.09
Square centimeters	Square inches	0.155
Square meters	Square feet	10.8
Square meters	Square yards	1.2
Cubic centimeters	Cubic inches	0.061
Cubic meters	Cubic feet	35.3
Cubic meters	Cubic yards	1.31
Milliliters	Ounces	.033
Liters	Pints (U.S.)	2.114 (Imp. 1.76)
Liters	Quarts (U.S.)	1.057 (Imp. 0.88)
Liters	Gallons (U.S.)	0.264 (Imp. 0.22)
Grams	Ounces	0.035
Kilograms	Pounds	2.2

Liquid Measurement Equivalents

1 Tablespoon		= 3 Teaspoons
1 Fluid Ounce		= 2 Tablespoons
1 Cup	= 8 Fluid Ounces	= 16 Tablespoons
1 Pint	= 16 Fluid Ounces	= 2 Cups
1 Quart	= 32 Fluid Ounces	= 2 Pints
1 Gallon	= 128 Fluid Ounces	= 4 Quarts

Calculating Room Dimensions

Wall height	= Distance from floor to ceiling
Wall length	= Distance from corner to corner
Square footage (area in feet)	
Wall	= Length × Height
Floor	= Length × Width
Ceiling	= Length × Width
Perimeter	= Length of all walls

Converting Temperatures

Convert degrees Fahrenheit (F) to degrees Celsius (C) by following this simple formula: Subtract 32 from the Fahrenheit temperature reading. Then, mulitply that number by ⅝. For example, 77°F - 32 = 45. 45 × ⅝ = 25°C.

To convert degrees Celsius to degrees Fahrenheit, multiply the Celsius temperature reading by ⅘. Then, add 32. For example, 25°C × ⅘ = 45. 45 + 32 = 77°F.

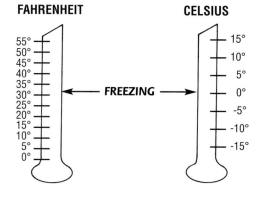

Abrasive Paper Grits - (Aluminum Oxide)

VERY COARSE	COARSE	MEDIUM	FINE	VERY FINE
12 - 36	40 - 60	80 - 120	150 - 180	220 - 600

Index

RESOURCES

The following manufacturers contributed photography and information for this book. For more information on their products, contact them at the addresses below.

Anaglypta/Lincrusta: pp. 262, 265 all
Crown House
Darwen, Lancashire England
tel: (44) 254-704-951
fax: (44) 254-760-700
http://www.anaglypta.com

Blonder Wallcoverings: pages 28, 32, 34, 36, 38, 42, 43
3950 Prospect Avenue
Cleveland, OH 44115
tel: 216-431-3560
fax: 216-431-5367
http://www.blonderwall.com

ORAC DECOR by Outwater Plastics Industries, Inc.: pages 278, 279, 281
Architectural Division
22 Passaic Street
Wood-Ridge, NJ 07075
tel: 800-631-8375
fax: 800-888-3315
http://www.outwater.com

Wagner Spray Tech Corp.:
pages 178, 180a
1770 Fernbroook Lane
Minneapolis, MN 55447
tel: 800-328-8251
fax: 612-509-7555
http://www.wagnerspraytech.com

Creative Publishing international, Inc. offers a variety of how-to books.
For information write or visit our website:
  Creative Publishing international, Inc.
  Subscriber Books
  5900 Green Oak Drive
  Minnetonka, MN 55343

www.howtobookstore.com